SHAKE THAT BRAIN!

SHAKE THAT BRAIN!

How to Create Winning Solutions

(and Have Fun While You're at It)

JOEL SALTZMAN

John Wiley & Sons, Inc.

Published by John Wiley & Sons, Inc., Hoboken, New Jersey.
Published simultaneously in Canada.

For general information on our other products and services or for technical support, please contact our Customer Care Department within the United States at (800) 762-2974, outside the United States at (317) 572-3993 or fax (317) 572-4002.

Wiley also publishes its books in a variety of electronic formats. Some content that appears in print may not be available in electronic books. For more information about Wiley products, visit our web site at www.wiley.com.

Library of Congress Cataloging-in-Publication Data:

Saltzman, Joel.
Shake that brain! : how to create winning solutions (and have fun while you're at it) / Joel Saltzman.
p. cm.
ISBN-13 978-0-471-74210-4 (cloth)
ISBN-10 0-471-74210-4 (cloth)
1. Creative ability in business. 2. Industrial management. I. Title.
HD53.S245 2006
650.1—dc22 2005026116

Printed in the United States of America

10 9 8 7 6 5 4 3 2 1

To create *anything* is to undergo the humbling and strange experience . . . of making something and *not knowing* where it comes from. It's as if the magician had no idea how the rabbit got into his hat.

—Francine Prose, *The Lives of the Muses*

Ideas are like rabbits. You get a couple and learn how to handle them, and pretty soon you have a dozen.

—John Steinbeck

Let's get some rabbits!

—Joel Saltzman

To my son, Miller—

Artist,
writer,
thinker,
singer extraordinaire,
and
the best darn pal
I ever had.

Contents

SHAKE THAT BRAIN!

Introduction

Shake That Brain!® is a powerful collection of creative and inspiring tips and tools for creating winning solutions—and having FUN while you're at it. These are skills you can use both professionally and personally—from marketing, innovation and product creation . . . to parenting, ethics, and personal growth.

As you'll soon discover, each *Shake That Brain!* strategy is backed by powerful and compelling examples from a wide variety of real-life applications—from "Worlds' Worst Pizza" and seeing-eye ponies . . . to why it can be a *good* idea to turn to your mate and say, "Shut up!"

Guaranteed: You'll be entertained AND enlightened—with plenty of energy, edge, and just plain FUN. Meanwhile, you'll learn to create surprising, yet inevitable solutions no matter the challenge or task at hand. Easily. Consistently. And economically.

Divided into three sections (*Attitude*, *Actions*, and *Selling*), *Shake That Brain!* will broaden your mindset, strengthen your upper-body solution-finding skills, and teach you to "sell" your solutions to key decision makers. You'll learn to:

- **Shake, rattle, and question your assumptions—they're crippling you!**

  That's what led Purina to develop "a unique litter training system"—for dogs.

- **Turn your worst ideas into GREAT ideas.**

  That's how Woolmark spread its message to eight million people without spending a penny on advertising.

- **Learn the power of "Opposites Thinking."**

  That's how Jeff Hawkins created the Palm Pilot.

- **Have "Yes" meetings only.**

  That's how Warner Bros. created its famous Looney Tunes cartoons with characters like Bugs Bunny and Daffy Duck.

- **Generate and implement bold new solutions—by using just what's in the room!**

  That's how NASA engineers fashioned a carbon dioxide filter out of duct tape, cardboard, and a sock for the troubled Apollo 13 spacecraft . . . how a businesswoman on the road fashioned a shower cap when there wasn't one . . . and how a lawyer reinvented herself, transforming her career "from something I hated to something I love."

- **Harness the Power of Proof (P.O.P.) to achieve maximum buy-in from buyers, bosses, and stakeholders.**

  That's how Edwin Land sold the American Optical Company on making its sunglasses with Polaroid lenses and how Richard Feynman sold fellow scientists, and the world, on his solution to a $50-million riddle.

Along the way, you'll learn to: ask great questions . . . never take "Yes" for an answer . . . turn any crisis into a great opportunity . . . and harness the brain power of experts for ZERO dollars a day. You'll get exercises, easy-to-apply formulas, entertaining pop quizzes, and eye-opening teaching examples from the world of business, technology, advertising, and more—all designed to make your reading experience both profitable *and* fun!

Who'll benefit most from this book? People in business (large or small) and people with a life *outside* of work. After all, whether it's business or the business of life, we're forever challenged to find creative solutions. So sit back, relax, and get ready to have more than a few laugh-out-loud moments while learning to *Shake That Brain!* Pretty soon, you'll have people saying to you, "Gee, why didn't I think of that!?"

Part One

ATTITUDE

– Or –

How to Prepare Your Brain for "New and Improved" Behavior

How important is attitude? It's the difference between *This is hopeless* and *This I can do!* One will get you nowhere; the other *everywhere* you want to go.

If your current mindset could use an adjustment, relief is just a page away: *Part One: Attitude* will prepare your brain for the fun ahead. If you already possess a *This I can do!* attitude, feel free to skip this section and move directly to *Part Two: Actions*. Regardless, your solution-finding success will depend on having the proper attitude—daring, playful, and wildly optimistic.

1

Be DARING

Allow yourself to look for wild, outlandish ideas and solutions, even if they seem impossible at first. As Einstein put it:

If at first an idea is NOT absurd, then there is no hope for it.

Yet at some point, we've all been guilty of saying—either out loud or to ourselves, "That's a crazy idea—forget it." To which we can imagine Einstein countering: "Got a crazy idea? Let's take a look!" The lesson? *Be daring!*

Dare to succeed, dare to fail. Dare to STICK OUT, dare to prevail. "Shake it, shake it, break it!"[1] "Take chances."[2] "Take the risk of breaking your neck."[3] "Be daring, be first, be different."[4]

1. **Jack Welch**
2. **Clint Eastwood**
3. **Picasso**
4. **Anita Roddick,** founder of Body Shop

As Bertrand Russell advised:

Do not fear to be eccentric in opinion, for every opinion now accepted was once eccentric.

What was "once eccentric"? *Just about everything.* The wheel. Books. Money. Democracy. Women's suffrage. Civil Rights. Cars. Planes. Computers. Everything you plug into the wall—and everything you *used* to plug in.

Whatever you can do or dream you can, begin it. Boldness has genius, magic and power in it. Begin it now.

—Goethe

What else do you get for daring to be bold? Detractors. But don't you worry: I'll show you how to show them the door.

2

Be PREPARED

Should you "dare" to be daring, one thing is sure: You will be ridiculed, belittled, laughed at, and worse.

"Foolish."
"Absurd."
"Sheer nonsense."

Such were the opinions of Sir William Preece, John T. Sprague, and Professor Silvanus Thompson, prominent minds in the field of electricity when Edison dared to create the light bulb. And the critics have never stopped.

Telephone?

No direct practical application.

—*The Telegrapher*, industry journal, 1870s

[T]oo many shortcomings to be seriously considered as a means of communication.

—Western Union Memo, 1876

Computer?

I think there is a world market for maybe five computers.

—Thomas J. Watson, founder of IBM (1943)

Personal Computer?

There is no reason for any individual to have a computer in their home.

—Ken Olson, former president, Digital Equipment (1977)

Another Invention???

Everything that can be invented has been invented.

—Charles H. Duel, director of Office of Patents (1899)

"All truth," wrote Schopenhauer, "passes through three stages. First it is ridiculed. Second, it is violently opposed. Third, it is accepted as self-evident." Or, as Mark Twain put it:

The man with a new idea is a crank until the idea succeeds.

Yet being called a "crank" (or worse) can also be viewed as something quite positive; a "bell weather" forecasting good things to come. As Ted Turner put it, "If you've got an innovative idea and the majority does not pooh-pooh it, then the odds are you must not have a very good idea." Turner should know; early doubters called fledgling CNN, "Chicken Noodle News."

Nuts, Insane & Disgusting

"My wife thought I was NUTS. She thought I was following in my father's footsteps . . . [Someone who was] always coming up with spectacular, impractical ideas." So confessed Jeff Hawkins, creator of the Palm Pilot. He warns: "If you're going to innovate . . . you're going to have all these people telling you you're wrong. . . . It takes a lot of nerve and perseverance. You have to keep fighting the battles."

Likewise, when Eli Wilner started collecting antique FRAMES (instead of paintings): "Everyone thought I was INSANE. From my parents to my art dealer friends to my present-day wife, everyone told me, 'This is the stupidest thing you'll ever do.' " Today, Eli Wilner & Company does about $3 million a year in business.

And when James Dyson was first shopping around his see-through Dyson Vacuums, retailers balked that seeing the accumulated dirt inside the vacuum was repulsive. Having had his idea roundly *pooh-poohed,* Dyson went on to clean up big.

Your own opposition—your personal pack of naysayers and doubters—may include bosses, coworkers, spouses, in-laws, and more. Having this book gives you the edge. Use it to (1) keep yourself going, (2) swat away opponents, or (3) stick it under their noses, pointing to where it says:

Great spirits have always encountered violent opposition from mediocre minds.

—Albert Einstein

"New opinions," wrote John Locke, "are always suspected, and usually opposed, without any other reason but because they are not already known."

Solution I: Keep it to yourself—at least until that initial idea has time to take clearer shape. Dilbert's creator, Scott Adams, has said that sometimes he'll have a great idea—then he makes the "mistake" of telling someone else. In fact, Adams turned his frustration into a memorable strip in which we see Dan, "the illogical scientist," telling a female coworker: "That idea won't work. I know because I've read many reports about ideas that didn't work." She complains, "You haven't even looked at my idea," to which Dan responds, "Oh, I get it; you're one of those religious nuts."

Solution II: When you do decide to spread the word, be careful who you tell. In 1952, Rear Admiral Grace Murray Hopper created the first computer compiler. Before then, creating new software meant starting from scratch. "Nobody believed it could be done," recalls Hopper. "Yet it was so obvious. Why start from scratch with every single program you write? Develop one that would do a lot of the basic work over and over again. Developing a compiler was a logical move; but in matters like this, you don't run against logic—you run against people who can't change their minds."

Mark Twain said it best: "Keep away from people who try to belittle your ambitions. Small people always do that, but the really great make you feel that you, too, can become great."

Solution III: Listen to the experts. (Sort of.) As science fiction writer Robert A. Heinlein advised, "Always listen to the experts. They will tell you what can't be done, and why. Then do it." Interestingly, Heinlein was most famous for his novel, *Stranger in a Strange Land*, a book that introduced the slang word "grok."

Literally, it means "to drink;" metaphorically "to be one with," to understand "in a profound and intimate way," as in the following comment from Apple cofounder and iPod champion, Steve Jobs: "Design is a funny word. Some people think design means how it looks. But, of course, if you dig deeper, it's really how it *works.* To design something really well, you have to 'get it'! You have to really grok what it's all about."

In the late 1950s, reports the *Los Angeles Times,* Forrest Ackerman, founder of the cult magazine *Famous Monsters of Filmland,* was "driving around with his wife when he heard someone on the radio say 'hi-fi.' He said to his wife, 'Why not sci-fi?' And, to her 'immortal embarrassment,' he reports, 'My wife said, "Forget it, Forrie. It will never catch on." ' "

POP QUIZ

When friends, family, fellow workers, or so-called experts fail to appreciate your new idea, it's because:

(a) They don't grok it.
(b) They don't want to grok it.
(c) They don't grok it because you failed to *sell* it. (See Part Three: Selling.)
(d) They consider it such an "intimidating challenge" they simply *refuse* to grok it.
(e) They're jealous of your superior intellect and outstanding good looks.

Nicholas V. Perricone, M.D., a dermatologist and author of the best-selling book *The Wrinkle Cure*, gets a lot of flack from the medical establishment. Coming to his own defense, Perricone told the *New York Times*: "It doesn't make anyone angry that dermatologists are injecting Botox or Restylane into people and making several million dollars a year in their practices. But let's complain about Perricone, who's recommending a balanced diet [with an emphasis on a lot of salmon, for essential fatty acids] . . . and using topicals rather than going for [injections or] cosmetic surgery." His detractors—and there are many—focus on his lack of controlled, peer-review data to back up his claims. How does Perricone take the heat? "Once, after I had given a lecture at a conference, a fellow scientist told me: 'I just want you to remember one thing. You can always recognize the pioneers by the number of arrows in their back.'" Pioneer, con-man, or both, Perricone is making a fortune. Literally. (In addition to having sold more than two million books, in 2004, sales of his skin care products line reached $50 million.)

If you stand up and be counted, from time to time you may get yourself knocked down. But remember this: A man flattened by an opponent can get up again. A man flattened by conformity stays down for good.

—Thomas J. Watson, founder of IBM

To be a champ you have to believe in yourself when nobody else will.

—Sugar Ray Robinson

CLASSICAL RIOT

Stravinsky's *The Rite of Spring* premiered at the Théâtre des Champs Elysées, in Paris, on May 29, 1913. In his book, *Music After the Great War,* Carl van Vechten, who was at the concert, reports: "A certain part of the audience, thrilled by what it considered to be a blasphemous attempt to destroy music as an art and swept away with wrath, began very soon after the rise of the curtain to whistle, to make catcalls, and to offer audible suggestions as to how the performance should proceed. Others of us who liked the music and felt that the principles of free speech were at stake bellowed defiance." Music historian Milton Cross, in his *Encyclopedia of the Great Composers and Their Music,* adds: "Hardly had the performance begun when Camille Saint-Saëns rose in his seat, made a bitter remark about the music, and left the theater with indignation. The critic André Capu yelled at the top of his lungs that the music was a colossal fraud; the Austrian ambassador laughed loudly in derision; the Princesse de Pourtalès left her box exclaiming, "I am sixty years old, but this is the first time that anyone dared to make a fool of me!" One lady reached out into the adjoining box and slapped the face of a man who was hissing; her escort arose, cards were exchanged, and a duel was arranged. A society lady rose majestically in her seat and spat in the face of one of the demonstrators. All the while, Maurice Ravel was shouting the word "genius"; another French composer and critic, Roland-Manuel, had the collar torn from his shirt because he defended the music, and he kept the collar as a precious memento ever after. Claude Debussy, pale and overwrought, was pleading with the audience around him to be silent and listen to the music. Backstage, Stravinsky held on to Nijinsky to prevent him from jumping into the audience and engaging in a fist fight with the obstreperous demonstrators."

Today, the music of "revolutionaries" like Stravinsky, Ravel, and Debussy forms the core of the 20th-century canon.

Miles Davis [was] booed.
Hank Williams was booed.
Stravinsky was booed.
You're nobody if you don't get booed sometimes.

—Bob Dylan

3

Be OPTIMISTIC

Optimism is key. Given a choice—and you are—decide to be like *The Little Engine That Could* ("I think I can, I think I can!"). In point of fact:

> **Whether you believe you CAN,**
> **or whether you believe you CAN'T,**
> **you're absolutely right.**
> —Henry Ford

What's required is courage: having the fear of failure AND the daring to move ahead despite uncertainty and doubt. "You're all by yourself in what feels like the middle of the ocean," writes surfer and novelist Kem Nunn. "You've gotten caught in the impact zone and you're being rolled by one wave after another. Your first impulse is to panic, to give up. But, of course, you can't give in to that." Are you in danger? *Yes*. Will you survive? *Depends how you look at it*.

Consider the following nearly *identical* ideas from mathematicians and philosophers René Descartes and Blaise Pascal:

An optimist may see light where there is none, but why must the pessimist always run to blow it out?

—Descartes

In faith there is enough light for those who want to believe and enough shadows to blind those who don't.

—Pascal

Whether you call it optimism or faith, the choice is the same—darkness or light. You can choose darkness: *Man, it's dark in here.* You can choose light: *There's light at the end of this tunnel.* Or you can choose both: *It's dark in here now but there WILL (I hope and pray) be light!*

Rollo May, in *The Courage to Create,* describes the "curious paradox" of courage as "the seeming contradiction that *we must be fully committed, but we must also be aware at the same time that we might possibly be wrong.*" He continues: "The relationship between commitment and doubt is by no means an antagonistic one. Commitment is healthiest when it is not *without* doubt, but *in spite of doubt.* To believe fully and at the same moment to have doubts is not at all a contradiction: it presupposes a greater respect for truth, an awareness that truth always goes beyond anything that can be said or done at any given moment."

Every movie I make, every movie I start, I don't think I can pull it off.

—Steven Spielberg

Courage is being scared to death—but saddling up anyway.

—John Wayne

ABBOT AND COSTELLO MEET THE WAITRESS

In an episode from the *Abbot and Costello* TV show (1952–1954), Bud and Lou sit at a lunch counter having only enough money for a sandwich and a cup of coffee for Bud. As Bud explains to Lou, "When the waitress asks you if you want anything, you say you don't want anything. Then when I get my sandwich I'll split it with you." After some initial misunderstandings—Bud puts on a show for the waitress, repeatedly encouraging Lou to "Go ahead, order something."—Lou catches on, telling their waitress, "I don't care for nothing." She exits through the swinging door to the kitchen. A moment later she returns, saying to Lou, "You're cute. . . . You can have a piece of cake on me." Lou accepts and all is well. Again, she exits through the swinging door. And again she comes right back, only this time she's *annoyed* at Lou for his having taken a piece of cake without asking. (Lou's confused, as is Bud.) She takes the cake away from him and heads back to the kitchen. A moment later, she returns again, only *this time* she doesn't understand why Lou isn't eating his cake. She gives him back the cake, *insisting* that he eat it. She exits, comes back, and is shocked to see Lou enjoying his cake.

It goes on like this, back and forth—*Enjoy it* v. *Leave it alone*—half a dozen times, each time Lou growing increasingly frustrated and confused. For us, the audience, that's part of the fun, watching as Lou keeps struggling, albeit unsuccessfully, to figure out *What the heck is going on here!?*

What the audience knows—but Bud and Lou don't—is that it's not *one* waitress, but a pair of twins, each one acting without the other one's knowledge.

What does Lou's frustration and confusion have to do with this book, you may ask? Plenty. What Lou goes through—vacillating between believing he *can't* have his cake and believing he *can*—is the difference, if you will, between "No, I *can't* find a great solution" and "Yes, I *can,* and will, get my just dessert." What it takes is *keeping the faith* despite all doubt, confusion, and radically opposing points of view.

Alternatively, forget Ford, Picasso, Descartes, Pascal, May, Abbot and Costello, and choose, instead, to heed the advice of songwriter and philosopher Johnny Mercer, who advised listeners to "*ac-cen-tu-ate the positive.*" Make that choice—decide to "*ac-cen-tu-ate the positive*"—and you become an optimist, someone who will lead a longer, healthier life and be better equipped to persevere when things are not going well. Or, as Voltaire put it, you will have a "mania for saying things are well when one is in hell." (If you are "in hell"—and I add this at the risk of gilding the lily—heed the advice of Churchill who said: "If you're going through hell, keep going.")

> What's the difference between a crisis and an opportunity? *Nothing*—if you're an optimist. If you're an optimist, a crisis is simply an *opportunity* waiting to happen. If you're a pessimist, an opportunity is a *crisis* waiting to happen. *(I got hired, I'll get fired.)*

4

Learn That MISTAKES Are GREAT

What "creative" people understand—better than anyone—is that mistakes are great. Mistakes, in fact, are the currency of creativity. "Creativity," says Dilbert creator, Scott Adams, "is allowing yourself to make mistakes. Art is knowing which ones to keep."

The math is simple: The more mistakes you make, the better your chances of success.

Back in my twenties, what I wanted most was to be a writer. Instead, I sentenced myself to five long years of writer's block. It was agony, my personal Dark Ages. Instead of writing, I spent my time worrying, going to therapy, and wondering if I'd one day finally have the courage to throw my typewriter out the window and myself right after it. Then one night, still in the throes of writer's block, I got a fortune cookie that saved my life. My fortune read:

TO AVOID BEING DISAPPOINTED, MINIMIZE EXPECTATIONS

Not being a true believer in the Fortune Cookie School of Wisdom, I was about to toss my fortune aside and never think of it again. But there was something about those words that almost made sense to me.

What if I did lower my expectations—*really* lowered them? What if I said to myself: *I don't care if it makes any sense or not. Whatever's in my head, I'm going to write it down.* That night, I started writing again, the same way I'd started out as a kid—just for the hell of it. I was fooling around again, having fun on the page, finger painting with words and ideas. I didn't care how crazy, or wild, or mistake-ridden it got. It got me going again and that's all that mattered.

And therein lies the secret to creative solutions. Whether you're creating a new product, working to solve a business problem, or trying to resolve a conflict with your children or spouse, what it takes is creativity—and that means mistakes.

That's not it.
That's not it.
That's not it.
Hey, that's it!

Some years ago, while in an airplane lavatory, I spotted two signs on the wall. The older sign read:

Please do not deposit anything other than toilet tissue in toilet.

The newer sign, just below, read:

Depositing objects other than toilet tissue in toilet could result in airplane failure.

Which sign would you say was the better solution?

That's not it.
That's not it.
That's not it.
Hey, that's it!

"Every strike," said slugger Babe Ruth, "brings me closer to the next home run." (In fact, the same year Ruth hit his then record-breaking sixty home runs he also led the league in strikeouts.) The path to success is simple and clear:

MINIMIZE EXPECTATIONS

Expect, instead, to be willing to fail, rethink, revise, and redirect. Constantly. "It's not that I'm smart," opined a humble Albert Einstein, "it's just that I stay with the problems longer."

In my own case, I learned to "stay with the problem" of writer's block until I stumbled upon the secret of my success: *Having the freedom to make mistakes*. Wrong turns, blind alleys, great ideas that don't pan out, and lousy ones that sometimes do. Eventually, I learned to *embrace* my mistakes, knowing, like the Babe, that every strike, every crumbled piece of paper, was bringing me that much closer to a real home run. (Or at least a single.)

Imagine your employer gave you a pair of dice and told you that in order to keep your job you had to roll a twelve. Your first reaction—aside from the obvious *Why?*—might well be fear. *How can I possibly guarantee I'll roll a twelve!?*

Your odds, in fact, are 100 percent. That's right, 100 percent. *Just keep rolling those dice . . . until you get a twelve!*

That's a six.
That's an eight.
That's a three.
That's a ten.
Hey, that's a twelve!

Tim Gill, cofounder of Quark publishing software, says: "The only way you learn what works is to learn what doesn't work." In other words: Mistakes. Twenty years after founding Quark, Gill sold his share of the company for $500 million.

Like to hit a home run, roll a twelve, or cash in your chips for $500 million? Let's get to work and start making mistakes!

TRUE STORY

When my father was in the Army, there was a private in his platoon who spent all his spare time searching for scraps of paper. He'd find a scrap, pick it up, examine both sides, then shake his head, "That's not it." This went on week after week. "That's not it. That's not it." Finally, they gave him a psychiatric exam and handed him his discharge. He looked it over, brightened, and said, "That's it!"

You never know when you're going to fail. That's just a part of succeeding—failing. And it's not that big of a deal. It's something to laugh about. You can pick yourself up and go on tomorrow. That's the beauty of it. That's how you succeed.

—Wynton Marsalis

Berry Gordy, creator of Motown Records (aka Hitsville) recalls in his autobiography, *To Be Loved,* "Hitsville had an atmosphere that allowed people to experiment creatively and gave them the courage not to be afraid to make mistakes. In fact, I sometimes encouraged mistakes."

Bottom line?

Mistakes are great!

Not only can mistakes lead us to better solutions, "mistakes," themselves, can actually work. In her very entertaining book, *Mistakes That Worked,* Charlotte Foltz Jones reviews "40 Familiar Inventions and How They Came to Be," including various icons of industry, like Coca Cola (someone accidentally added carbonated water instead of regular water), Ivory Soap (someone else accidentally allowed air into the mixture, producing the "soap that floats"), Scotchguard (an accidental spill on a tennis shoe wound up keeping that spot only nice and clean), the vulcanization of rubber (it spilled on a stove), Silly Putty (a "failed" rubber substitute), and Post-it Notes (made from a "failed" adhesive we'll learn more about later in the chapter, "Get Support for It"). As Mark Twain wrote in his notebook, "Name the greatest of all inventors. Accident."

5

Have FUN with It

Most of all, problem solving—and solution finding—is a game. The process can be grueling and dreadful or—as "absurd" as this sounds—it can be fun. In other words:

Ya gotta have FUN.

Why? Because fun reduces stress, loosens us up, and gets and keeps our creative juices flowing. Daniel Goleman, in his book *Emotional Intelligence* writes: "Good moods, while they last, enhance the ability to think flexibly and with more complexity, thus making it easier to find solutions to problems, whether intellectual or interpersonal."

In fact, says Goleman, a "good laugh" comes in handy when "solving a problem that demands a creative solution." He explains: "One study found that people who had just watched a video of television bloopers were better at solving a puzzle long used by psychologists to test creative thinking. In the test, people are given a candle, matches, and a box of tacks and asked to attach the candle to a corkboard wall so it will burn without dripping wax on the floor. Most people given this problem fall into 'functional fixedness,' thinking about using the objects in the most conventional ways. But those who had just watched the funny film, compared to others who had watched a film on math or who exercised, were more likely to see an alternative use for the box holding the tacks, and so come up with the creative solution: tack the box to the wall and use it as a candleholder."

"I like nonsense," said Dr. Seuss, "it wakes up the brain cells."

Jane and Michael Stern, in *Jane & Michael Stern's Encyclopedia of POP Culture,* tell the following story: "Gary Dahl, a California advertising man, was having drinks with his buddies one night in April 1975 when the conversation turned to pets. As a lark, Mr. Dahl informed his friends that he considered dogs, cats, birds, and fish all a pain in the neck. They made a mess; they misbehaved; they cost too much money. He, on the other hand, had a pet rock, and it was an ideal pet—easy and cheap, and it had a great personality. His buddies started to riff with the off-the-wall idea and pretty soon they were all tossing around the notion of a pet rock and all the things it was good for.

Dahl debuted the Pet Rock at gift shows in San Francisco and New York. "Neiman Marcus ordered five hundred. . . . *Newsweek* did a half-page story about the nutty notion," and, within a few months, people purchased a million rocks for $3.95 apiece. "Gary Dahl—who decided from the beginning to make at least one dollar from every rock—had become an instant millionaire."

TRUE STORY

Realizing he could make some easy money through recycling, my son (nine at the time) started collecting empty cans and bottles in shopping bags in our garage. Eventually, with my wife and I running out of space to park our cars, it was time to visit the recycling center. It was a Sunday, it was hot, and I didn't want to go. But for the sake of my son—and our planet—we packed up the car and off we went. The ride over was smelly enough, as the fermenting aromas of beer, soda, and various leftovers soon filled our car. I'd never been to a recycling center but I was not looking forward to it. All I wanted was for our trip to be over.

The "recycling center," we discovered, was a simple, no-frills operation: A smelly, dirty man in a smelly, dirty shed, flanked by two self-operating machines on either side. The machines, which looked like soda vending machines in reverse, would take our empties, one by one, and keep a tally of our earnings—from 5 cents for a can to 10 cents for a larger bottle.

Suddenly, it hit me: I told my son we'd have a contest—see who could rack up the most money the fastest. He'd take one machine, I'd take the other. And no matter who won, he'd get to keep all the money.

Turning our work into a *game,* we had some real dad-and-son fun—even if it was a recycling center—and finished up in record time. The winner? Both of us: for finishing up fast—and having fun. Because FUN keeps you young (and, in this case, got me home and showered in record time).

The most creative people I know . . . [refuse] to do anything they don't want to do. That doesn't mean they never do unpleasant tasks. But they manage to transform even those tasks into something that comes closer to their interest. "I have worked every minute of my life," creative people say. "And I never did a lick of work in my life." Both statements are true.

—Mihaly Csikszentmihalyi

The idea is to die young as late as possible.

—Dr. Ashley Montagu (1905–1999)

POP QUIZ

What do you call a business where dogs roam free, there are roller-hockey games in the corridors (filled with Lava lamps, beanbag chairs, and hammocks), you can play shuffleboard, Ping Pong, pool, and arcade games, there's a gym, including saunas, full-time masseuses, yoga classes, free Ben & Jerry's bars, and employees get a free healthy lunch every day, once prepared by the former chef of the Grateful Dead?

Answer:

Google corporate headquarters in Mountain View, California, where fun AND profits go hand in hand. Today, among the "Top 10 Reasons to Work at Google," their Web site promises: ". . . a fun and inspiring workplace [where] work and play are not mutually exclusive. It is possible to code and pass the puck at the same time . . . Innovation is our bloodline. . . . [You will] boldly go where no one has gone before [and] there is such a thing as a free lunch after all. In fact, we have them every day: healthy, yummy, and made with love."

Humanity has advanced, when it has advanced, not because it has been sober, responsible, and cautious, but because it has been playful, rebellious, and immature.

—Tom Robbins

Fun Factoids

1. The name *Google*—which is **FUN** to say and clearly adds to the company's appeal—comes from the word "googol," the number 1 followed by 100 zeros. That is:

10,000,000,000,000,000,000,000,000,000,000,000,000,000,
000,000,000,000,000,000,000,000,000,000,000,000,
000,000,000,000,000,000,000,000,000

2. How did *Google* get its name? Company cofounder Larry Page explains that in addition to it being "short" and "reasonably easy to spell," "it was fun." There's that word again: **FUN.**

The supreme accomplishment is to blur the line between work and play.

—Arnold J. Toynbee

THE F-WORD

An "expert" in the field of fun is Burt Rutan, legendary airplane designer and CEO of Scaled Composites, an aerospace operation with more than 100 employees. As Rutan told the *Los Angeles Times Magazine* in 1999: "If you're having fun, you're more likely to be productive. . . . By putting the f-word up front, I've been able to attract talented people to work here even though they could make as much, if not more at, say, Lockheed or Boeing. Having fun is how I've managed to create a profitable company. . . . In the last five years, we've done four new-from-scratch airplanes . . . and I don't think that's good enough. I think we ought to be doing something more fun, something more challenging."

Five years later, in 2004, Scaled Composites won the Ansari X-Prize for becoming the first private company to launch a man into space and bring him back safely. Twice, in fact, within the same week. Rutan's state of mind since winning the prize? According to Chief engineer Matthew Gionta, as reported in *Inc.* magazine: "He's like a kid in a candy store. He's having more fun than he ever has." (Oh, and the X-Prize includes a $10 million check.)

Still not convinced of the power of fun? Tattoo the **f-word** on your forehead (be sure to do it backwards), then look in the mirror and repeat after Burt:

"We ought to be doing something more fun!
We ought to be doing something more fun!
We ought to be doing something more fun!"

(Repeat this mantra until it really sinks in.)

Fun AND Profits? Absolutely!

Around 1990, Mike Veeck purchased six minor league baseball teams for less than $2 million. Believing that "fun is a basic human need," Mike Veeck began a mission to inject as much FUN into the ballpark experience as possible: having the grounds crew drag the infield *in drag,* getting pigs to deliver baseballs to the umpire, and, on Bat Day, giving away inflatable bats imprinted with the word *Viagra.* (Oh, and on Labor Day, pregnant women get in free.) As Veeck writes in his book, *Fun is Good*: "Our philosophy begins and ends with the notion that fun is good. That applies to not only the product we're selling—a family-oriented evening at the ballpark full of laughter, zany promotions, wacky stunts, and free giveaways—but also our office environment. We have fun at work. We enjoy what we do, and that rubs off on our customers, who leave our ballparks not only entertained but feeling good about themselves and our product." Son of the late Hall of Fame club owner Bill Veeck, he says his father "understood people, and that when they had fun, they would spend money." And so they have. According to Veeck, his passion for fun has helped turn his $2 million investment "into a roughly $25 million annual business," with assets valued at nearly $30 million.

In the movie *Master and Commander* (2003), Captain Jack Aubrey (Russell Crowe) takes a similar approach to the importance of **FUN**—even in the midst of battle: With his ship under fire, Captain Jack orders his crew to craft a makeshift decoy. He then sends a young officer off by himself to sail the decoy away from their ship. Dodging cannon fire, the young man gets the decoy on its way, then swims back to the ship. Hoisted aboard, his smiling Captain greets him with the words: "Now tell me that wasn't **FUN**!"

Free BRAIN SURGERY!

Results Guaranteed.

"Haven't lost a patient yet!"

Richard Branson, who captains more than 300 companies (with more than $8 billion a year in sales) puts it like this: "If the chairman's having fun, it's easier for everyone else. And if it's fun, you're going to keep going until you drop."

Like Chairman Richard and Captain Jack, I'm always looking to keep **FUN** in my lessons. In my *Shake That Brain!* programs, for example, part of the fun comes from my performing free, on-stage brain surgery.

Likewise, when I was invited to be part of Nutrition Week at my son's grade school, I decided to have to have some FUN with it. So I showed up as "Bobo-the-Baker," teaching the benefits of whole wheat breads and pastas by adding new lyrics to the song, "He's Got the Whole World in His Hands." That way, we could all sing together:

I've got the whole-wheat in my bread,
I've got the whole-wheat in my bread,
I've got the whole-wheat in my bread,
I've got the whole-wheat in my bread!

Not only did we have lots of fun, kids went home and sang it to their parents. And many who had been white bread loyalists, I've been told, suddenly demanded whole wheat bread for *all* future sandwiches.

Unfortunately, many people fear that being productive and having fun are at odds with each other. To them, the word "fun" really *is* the f-word. As adults, they figure it's their job to be as **SERIOUS** as possible. (Or so goes the party line.) Yet **FUN**, as we've seen, can serve some very useful **FUN**ctions:

1. It helps us create more creative solutions.
2. It can be profitable, as more "creative" solutions are often the most cost-effective.
3. It make us feel better, leading to overall improved health and decreased absenteeism.

4. It helps us to learn. (Yesterday, when I picked my son up from school, half a dozen kids started singing the whole-wheat bread song. It happens all the time—even though my appearance as "Bobo-the-Baker" was nearly a year ago.)

   And yes, adults can have fun AND learn as well.

Consider the following two approaches to conveying the importance of properly washing your hands to rid them of germs, especially during flu season:

Approach #1: Using warm water and soap, wash your hands for fifteen seconds. That is longer than you think; try counting slowly to fifteen next time you wash up and you'll see how deficient the average two-second rinse really is.

Approach #2: Using warm water and soap, wash your hands while singing the ABC's, concluding with: "*Now I know my ABC's, next time won't you sing with me.*" Or try ending your song with: "*Now I've washed my hands so well, take a look and have a smell.*" Or make up your own lyrics. Just remember to sing your ABC's *all the way through.* That should take you about fifteen seconds—all the time you need for a good and proper hand washing job.

Question: Which lesson seems like more **FUN** to you? And which, do you think, you're more likely to follow?

"Now tell me that wasn't FUN!"

6

Don't Feel Like a NINCOMPOOP

While highly desirable, prized, and rewarded, extraordinary solutions are not that easy to come by—which is why they're called **EXTRA**ordinary.

That's not it.
That's not it.
That's not it.
That's it!

While going through your *That's not it!* phase—including wrong turns, blind alleys, and plain dumb mistakes—be prepared to question your sanity, intellect, and powers of persistence. Then brush yourself off and get back to work—all the time reminding yourself:

**No matter how I feel,
I am not now
(nor have I ever been)
a nincompoop.**

Part Two

ACTIONS

– Or –

How to Shake Those New Ideas Loose

As promised in the Preface, this book contains "a powerful collection of creative and inspiring tips and tools for creating winning solutions—and having FUN while you're at it." Well, here they are—presented as a series of Actions you can take to create winning solutions.

Unlike a recipe, you do *not* need to follow each step in order. (Though you certainly can.) What I suggest is that first you read each chapter—in the order it's presented. Then return to the *start* of Part Two with a specific problem or question in mind. That's when you can pick and choose various "tips and tools" as a way for discovering those great solutions. Though there is one tool I suggest you begin with, regardless of the task at hand, *Question Your Assumptions.*

7

Question Your ASSUMPTIONS

How do you get a "winning" idea, or open your mind to new solutions? First, clear the deck of your OLD ideas by challenging your assumptions—everything you "know to be true" about your product, service, industry or problem du jour. No matter how logical, gotta-be-true, no-doubt-about-it your assumption, stop—ask yourself if maybe it "ain't necessarily so." After all, what's tried and true may, in fact, be tired and false.

In *The Affluent Society,* economist John Kenneth Galbraith wrote that new ideas "need to be tested" against the "inertia and resistance" of "conventional wisdom." That is: what everyone *knows to be true* may, in fact, not be true at all. The problem, believed Galbraith, is "We associate truth with convenience—with what most closely accords with self-interest and personal well-being or promises best to avoid awkward effort or unwelcome dislocation of life. . . . Therefore, we adhere, as though to a raft, to those ideas which represent our understanding"—even if our understanding is limited at best.

"Conventional wisdom," adds fellow economist, Steven D. Levitt in *Freakonomics,* "is often shoddily formed and devilishly difficult to see through, but it can be done." He continues: "It would be silly to argue that the conventional wisdom is *never* true. But noticing where the conventional wisdom may be false—noticing, perhaps, the contrails of sloppy or self-interested thinking—is a nice place to start asking questions."

MAJOR LEAGUE BASEBALL

In my days playing Little League, our coach was forever telling us, "A walk's as good as a hit." Because I was not a good hitter—and because most of the pitchers we faced threw more balls than strikes—I took his advice to heart and wound up getting on base a lot. (Not many hits, mind you, but I was convinced my coach was right: "A walk *is* as good as a hit!")

Back home, though, watching professional baseball games on TV, what I never understood was why big league statistics only gave a player credit for getting on base as the result of a hit, not for a walk. To me—a veteran walker at the age of ten—it just didn't seem fair. (Or very smart.) It still doesn't.

Consider two players, A and B. Player A, for every three trips to the plate, gets one hit and strikes out twice. He's said to have a .333 batting average. (In fact, a very good average.) In contrast, Player B strikes out once and draws two walks. His average is .000. *Zero!* Clearly, Player A has the better average, even though Player B gets on base TWICE as often. (To make up for this statistical oversight, or "error," I'd mentally recalculate each player's average, awarding, in this case, Player B a getting-on-base "average" of .666. *Major League Baseball just didn't get it.*)

Meanwhile, a player's batting average had always been used to determine the "value" of a player's hitting ability—and, consequently, became a measure of what a team would be willing to pay for his services. The "value" of a walk—contrary to logic, but fully in line with conventional wisdom—was Zero.

As Michael Lewis explains in *Moneyball,* the concept of walks not being credited to the batter was a holdover from the earliest days of baseball, when Henry Chadwick, an Englishman, set about "counting the events that occurred on a ball field." This included, Chadwick's decision "that walks were caused entirely by the pitcher—that the hitter had nothing to do with them. . . . 'There is but one true criterion of skill at the bat,' he wrote, 'and that is the number of times bases are made on clean hits.' "

Chadwick, however, was dead bang wrong, as proven by amateur statisticians Bill James and Voros McCracken. The world of baseball, they discovered, "placed too much value on batting average" and "didn't place enough value on walks."

Look at it this way: Each time a pitcher throws a ball the batter has a choice—either let it go and wait for a better pitch, or try to hit the ball. And that choice exists whether the pitcher throws a strike, or throws a ball. So it's not just the pitcher who determines whether a pitch is a ball, it's also the batter's "eye"—his ability to judge, within a fraction of a second, whether he should swing at a particular pitch, or let it go—that contributes to whether the umpire calls it a "ball." (There's also the individual *umpire's* "eye" that plays a factor, but that's a discussion for another time.) Bottom line? The batter plays an important role in whether or not he *earns* a base on balls.

In lieu of "batting average" (the percentage of times a batter earns a hit), James and McCracken suggested a far more appropriate measure of a batter's worth—his "on base average," including those times he gets on base as the result of a walk. The "value" of a walk, they argued—contrary to conventional wisdom, but fully in line with logic—could not possibly be Zero. A walk, in fact, deserved to be valued the *same* as a hit. Whether a batter gets to base from a hit or a walk, the result is the same—bringing his team that much closer to scoring a run—hence their conviction that "batting average" should be replaced with "on base average," a clearly superior measure of a batter's worth.

"The fetish made of 'runs batted in'," writes Lewis, "was another good example of the general madness. RBI had come to be treated by baseball people as an individual achievement—free agents were *paid* for their reputation as RBI machines when clearly they were not. . . . Why did they get so much credit for this? To knock runners in, runners needed to be on base when you came to bat. There was a huge element of luck in even having the opportunity, and what wasn't luck was, partly, the achievement of others. 'The problem,' wrote James, 'is that baseball statistics are not pure accomplishments of men against other men, which is what we are in the habit of seeing them as. They are accomplishments of men in combination with their circumstances.' "

What it took to put these theories into practice was Oakland A's general manager, Billy Beane, who quickly realized that James and McCracken were as right as Chadwick had been wrong—that certain time-honored baseball values did not hold up under scrutiny and that it was well past time to apply a new math to the valuation of players. Moreover, Beane was in desperate need for help. During the late 1990s, while player salaries were skyrocketing, Beane had meager resources—"working with either the lowest or the second lowest payroll in the game" (only one-third as much as the New York Yankees, the richest team). Determined to make the most of his very limited budget, Beane was able to buy, or trade for, enough *undervalued* players to make a huge difference in his team's performance—winning "more regular season games than any other team, except the Atlanta Braves," having gotten "to the play-offs three years in a row and in the previous two [years] taken the richest team in baseball, the Yankees, to within a few outs of elimination [with only one-third the payroll budget]. How on earth had they done that? . . . How [in 1999] did the second poorest team in baseball, opposing ever greater mountains of cash, stand even the faintest chance of success, much less the ability to win more regular season games than all but one of the other twenty-nine teams?"

1. They questioned assumptions.
2. They determined that various time-honored metrics did not hold up under scrutiny.
3. As a result of no one *else* having done 1 and 2, they were able to invest their limited resources on players who were clearly undervalued.

MAJOR LEAGUE CRIME

In his book, *Leadership,* Rudy Giuliani recalls: "When I ran for mayor in 1993, I promised to do something about the out-of-control crime rates that were holding the city hostage. . . . I didn't want to tinker with the police department, I wanted to revolutionize it. . . . I wanted to challenge every assumption about urban policing, issue a 'why not?' to every single 'That's not how it's done.' " Once in office, he assembled "about 500 people into twelve teams, each assigned to envision a police force with no preconceptions."

What Giuliani calls the "centerpiece" of these efforts was, like Beanes's, based in statistics. "A main frustration with the state of policing" had been "that each set of [crime] statistics was already obsolete by the time it was available. Examining the numbers annually or even quarterly wasn't accomplishing anything in real time. By the time a pattern of crime was noticed, it would have changed."

Rudy's revolution? Let's collect and analyze crime statistics *every single day* on a precinct by precinct basis, "to recognize patterns and potential trouble before it spreads." At the time, "No Police Department anywhere was gathering data with that frequency, and I felt it would take two or three years to implement." Yet, *three weeks later* Compstat's "first numbers rolled out of the station houses."

Within twelve months, Compstat, along with other measures, helped reduce crime citywide: major felonies down 12.3 percent; murder, 17.9 percent; and robbery, 15.5 percent. ("While it was true that crime was falling nationwide," adds the ex-Mayor, somewhat defensively, "New York's crime reduction was three to six times the national average.") In 1996, the city had further confirmation. Compstat won Harvard's Innovation in Government Award.

Don't run a city or major league ball club? You can still make a difference by questioning assumptions—regardless of your field.

For example . . .

Assumption: When people use a stapler, they leave it on their desk.

Maybe yes, maybe not often. Inspired by research that indicated that 80 percent of Americans pick up their staplers to use them, in 1997 Hunt Manufacturing Co. debuted a new kind of stapler, designed with an ergonomic grip and intended for hand-held use. Not only did questioning an assumption—*Do people use their stapler while it sits on their desk?*—lead to multiple awards for the hand-held design, it also brought new attention and incremental sales to an otherwise flat market. Meanwhile, Hunt questioned another assumption—*Must staplers lie lengthwise on a desk?* Realizing there wasn't a rule, per se, Hunt decided to make its new stapler—the Boston StandUP—stand vertically, ready to be gripped and put to use. It takes up less room, looks like a small piece of art, and neatly sets itself apart from the crowd. (For another example of a "vertical not horizontal" solution, consider the BeoCom telephone from Bang & Olufsen, with a handset that stands *vertically* on the desk.)

Assumption: Home buyers want basements.

Mr. Homebuilder, you sure about that? According to surveys by KB Home, when given a choice many buyers prefer doing without a basement. Losing a basement dramatically cuts costs and benefits both builder and buyer. Glen Barnard, KB's division president in Colorado, admits: "The preferences about basements were probably there for years, but we never bothered to ask." *Ask questions, learn about life—specifically yours.*

Assumption: You can't let people return used cosmetics.

At Rite Aid you can. When Rite Aid introduced its money-back guarantee, cosmetic sales shot up by about 25 percent—more than offsetting the occasional return.

Assumption: A credit card is the shape and size of, well, a credit card.

Until 2002 that was true. That's when Discover Bank broke a time-honored mold by introducing its Discover 2GO Card. Shaped like a painter's pallet, it features its own protective case, even a key-ring option. (Ever leave home without your wallet? If you took your keys, you're still in the money—assuming you signed up for a Discover 2GO Card.)

Assumption: Vodka is clear.

Introducing Blavod vodka, double-filtered, triple-distilled, and totally black. At Flints, a supper club in Santa Monica, California, owner Dodd Harris explains: "People wear black in this town—it's the color they use to project their power."

What's next, a credit card in black? Actually, American Express already has one. Considered by some the ultimate status symbol, the black card, with no credit limit, is offered to customers on an "invitation only" basis. You can't even apply for one. One just shows up in your mailbox one day. (Or it doesn't.)

Assumption: When designing a restaurant, lighting is important.

While this may be true nearly 100 percent of the time, still, it "ain't necessarily so." Welcome to Invisible, Berlin's no-lights, no-sights restaurant. Here, patrons are escorted to their tables by blind waiters. And the entire meal is served—and enjoyed—in the dark.

Assumption: At a casino, security guards—unless undercover—should be dressed as security guards.

A no-brainer, perhaps? Not for Steve Wynn. At Wynn's Caesar's Palace, the figures standing guard are security GLADIATORS.

Assumption: **It's important for a country to know its GNP.**

Yet Richard Layard, an economic adviser to Tony Blair from 1997 to 2001, argues that we ditch GNP in favor of measuring a county's "subjective well-being." That is, its happiness. *Crazy,* you say? In his book, *Happiness,* Layard offers the example of the Himalayan kingdom of Bhutan (population 1.1 million), which calculates its yearly objectives not in terms of GNP, but GNH (Gross National Happiness).

> **[C]reative people . . . are as curious, engaged, and innocent as children. They keep asking questions, wrestling with interesting problems, looking at the world through an ever-changing lens.**
>
> —Mihaly Csikszentmihalyi

HOW TO CHALLENGE THOSE STAPLER ASSUMPTIONS

Let's say you're a manufacturer who's impressed by the example of the StandUP Stapler and you want to create a new kind of stapler. First, make a list of everything you "know to be true" about staplers. No matter how "obvious" the assumption, write it down. For example:

1. They use staples.
2. When they run out of staples, you need to put new ones in.
3. They lie flat on a desk—until recently, that is.

Having listed every assumption you can think of, now go back and challenge each assumption.

1. Do staplers have to use staples?
2. What if you had a stapler with an endless supply of staples? Or a stapler that was disposable: you just threw it out when it ran out of staples?

That's how you do it. You list each assumption, then rigorously challenge each of your assumptions—no matter how obvious the given or ridiculous the alternative.

Let's look at our first assumption: "Staplers use staples." Here's a given that's so obvious on its face, what can you say but: *Of course they use staples!*

Now stop—ask yourself if maybe it "ain't necessarily so."

"A stapler that doesn't use staples?" you ask, "How can that be?"

Easy—with the Staple Free Stapler from Made By Humans. How does it work? It cuts out tiny tabs of paper that cleverly fold over and clasp together. ("Never run out of staples again—ever!") A neat little trick that began by questioning a most basic assumption: *Must staplers use staples?*

"The problem," says Visa founder Dee Hock, "is never how to get new innovative ideas into your mind—but how to get the old ones out." Rid yourself of assumptions—*Of course staplers use staples!*—and new ideas have a chance to emerge.

I have learned throughout my life as a composer chiefly through my mistakes and pursuits of false assumptions, not my exposure to fonts of wisdom and knowledge.

—Igor Stravinksy

I can't understand why people are frightened of new ideas. I'm frightened of the old ones.

—John Cage

TRUE STORY

In 2003 Staples held a contest to solicit product ideas from its customers. Out of 8,300 entries, Todd Basche won the contest by questioning a basic assumption about combination locks. Instead of assuming—like the rest of the world—that combination locks depended on dials or tumblers labeled with *numbers,* his idea was to use *letters* instead.

Why letters? With letters, you can use easy-to-remember code words to unlock your WordLock. Mr. Basche's reward? $25,000, plus royalties.

Now really? How tough was that to figure out!?

True, Basche could simply have had a spontaneous brainstorm while crossing the street one day. Or, he could have arrived at his winning idea by following three simple steps:

1. Consider an everyday product. A combination lock, for example. Or one of your own products or services.
2. Make a list of everything you can think of you absolutely know-to-be true about that product or service.
3. Go back and QUESTION each and every assumption.
4. (Optional) Submit to Staples and collect $25,000.

Hypothetical Writing Assignment #1

Imagine you're a copywriter in charge of drafting the words on the label of new bottled water. What are your ASSUMPTIONS about what to say? And can you CHALLENGE those assumptions to arrive at a "new" solution?

Following are examples from three bottled waters currently on the market. See which words appeal to YOU the most.

Norm's Mountain Spring Water *Clear bottle. Clean taste.*

Arrowhead Mountain Spring Water *Since 1894. Arrowhead Mountain Spring Water comes to you exclusively from natural mountain sources in the United States and Canada, giving it a clean, crisp and refreshing taste.*

Glacéau smartwater (nutrient enhanced water) *Vapor distilled + electrolytes. Side effects may include being called nerd, dork, geek, dweeb, brainiac, know-it-all, smarty-pants, smart-aleck, bookworm, egghead, four-eyes, Einstein, or being mistaken for the I.T. guy. May induce sudden and inexplicable aversion to all less intelligent forms of water. Apply liberally and frequently to dry people.*

That's the first part of the label. There's also a sidebar:

Your brain on glacéau ***smart****water.*

As you drink more and more water—progressively lowering the water level—the indicator reads (top to bottom) from "capable" to:

kinda arid
electrolytes flowing
clever enough
getter there (nice and moist)
witty
85% hydrated
genius (mensa material)

Question 1: You spot all three bottles on your grocer's shelves, each priced exactly the same. Which do you choose?

Question 2: Smartwater is priced just one penny more. Do you STILL consider buying it?

Question 3: How many MORE pennies could smartwater add and still get you to favor their product?

Question 4: Regardless of price, does smartwater's label help it to stand apart from the crowd?

If you think smartwater's label is unique, consider the labels for Dr. Bronner's Magic Soaps. Filled with quotes, predictions, and pleas for peace, his soap labels achieved icon status in the 60s and 70s—and they're still very much around today. (For sample labels, go to: http://www.drbronner.com/story.html#labels.) Today, Dr. Bronner's give-'em-a-piece-of-your-mind label philosophy carries over to a variety of "health-oriented" products—from Celestial Seasonings' gentle words on "Learning to Pause" while enjoying a cup of their tea to the tongue-in-cheek rants of Col. P. L. "Pops" Newman on Newman's Own Old Style Picture Show Microwave Popcorn. Ranting aside, Newman's most compelling copy is this: "Over $100 Million Given to Over 2,000 charities since 1982. Paul Newman donates all profits, after taxes, from the sale of this product for educational and charitable purposes." How's that for a claim of distinction?

Hypothetical Writing Assignment #2

Having graduated from writing for bottled water, a hotel chain asks you to submit your ideas for "Do Not Disturb" door hangers. Clearly, not what you'd call a sexy assignment—unless you're determined to somehow improve on the tried and true. For example, instead of the traditional "Do Not Disturb" sign in English, followed by the same message in different languages, consider the following real-life examples, collected from my travels:

> From the Sheraton Hotels, a door hanger that politely requests, "No surprises, please." (And just to be sure, in smaller letters below: "Do Not Disturb.")
>
> From the House of Blues Hotel, an in-your-face, "Do My Room" on one side, "Don't Bother Me" on the other.
>
> And my personal favorite, from the Hard Rock Hotel in Las Vegas . . . "I Hear Ya Knockin' But Ya Can't Come In!"

MORE ASSUMPTIONS TO TEST YOUR "UNCONVENTIONAL WISDOM" IQ

Assumption: When you sign up for a supermarket discount "club" card and they ask you to fill in your name and address—you have to fill in the truth.

What if you don't like giving out personal information but still want a card? Question your assumptions and you can get that card without losing your anonymity. My own card is registered to John Doe, who lives at 1 Main Street, Anywhere, USA. John's Zip code? 12345. (But here's the kicker. After I filled out my John Doe application, the cashier told me she had to get it "approved" by her manager. *Uh, oh,* I thought. *The jig is up*. For a moment, I considered saying something like, "Let me have that application back. I think maybe I made a spelling mistake." But before I knew it, her manager came over, glanced at my application, and approved it on the spot.

Assumption: In 2000, five architectural firms were asked to compete for the same assignment: How to spend $200 million to unify six seemingly unrelated structures comprising the Los Angeles County Museum of Art (LACMA).

In direct OPPOSITION to the assignment, competitor Rem Koolhaas began his presentation by reportedly saying: "Look, anything that begins with the words 'link' or 'unite' is doomed to failure. You are not going to get anything good if you take this approach, so I am throwing it out." Rather than "unite" the buildings, Koolhaas' solution was to destroy four of them and begin anew—without breaking the budget. Not only did Koolhaas ignore the competition rules . . . he also got the job. (Necessary but unfortunate update, 2005: Due to problems with funding, rumors of competing architects crying foul, or both, the fate of the project is murky, possibly dead.)

> **Keep the options open in everything you do. You don't learn by drawing a line in the sand and saying these are the limits.**
>
> —Bono, U2

Assumption: The place to post an Exit sign is above the doorway.

Yet on 9/11, many Pentagon workers had trouble seeing those signs as they kept low to the floor to avoid the smoke. Today, there are Exit signs at the Pentagon just six inches from the floor.

Assumption: If you operate your business out of an industrial park, you need to adhere to the same rules for signage as everyone else.

According to your lease, that's probably true. Yet eyewearhouse—where I get my glasses—seems to *bend* those rules (each and every morning) by planting bright yellow signs in the lawn—starting at the roadway about 50 yards off and leading (big surprise!) all the way to their doorway. Until someone objects, I suspect they'll keep planting their signs . . . and keep reaping the profit. (In fact, it was *because* of those signs that I discovered them in the first place.)

Assumption: Quarterly dividends need to be paid, well, quarterly.

The problem for Disney was how to reduce the cost of mailing those quarterly checks to its 1.7 million shareholders—many of whom own just a few shares—resulting in processing and postage costs that were often greater than the dividend payment inside. Disney's 1999 solution? Pay dividends to smaller shareholders on an annual basis instead of quarterly.

Assumption: If your spouse suffers from chronic back pain and you want him to feel better—as opposed to hurting the one you love—be solicitous, say comforting things.

According to research by neuropsychologist Herta Flor, that assumption, though well-meaning, is entirely wrongheaded. In fact, when you pay too much attention to someone's pain, it makes their experience of that pain not less, but *more*. Want your complaining spouse to feel better? (1) Change the subject, or (2) Ignore him.

Assumption: You're back in the supermarket, now facing a sign that reads:

Deluxe Mixed Nuts: 3/$10
Regular Price: $4.79

You Must Buy 3 to Save!

Clearly, there's a significant savings to be had—assuming you're willing to buy three cans. Question your assumptions, however, and you may discover, as I did, that when you purchase just one can you still get the savings, paying just $3.34—regardless of what the sign says.

Now before we leave the supermarket, let's take one more look at that sign for Deluxe Mixed Nuts. It invites us to assume we must make an archetypal **Either/Or** choice: "**Either** I buy three cans (and save money) **or** I buy one can (and I don't save money)." Yet, as we've already learned, there's also a **third** choice: "I can buy one can and still save money."

The moment you find yourself thinking your choice is "Either X or Y" . . . **STOP**. Recognize that you are a victim of Either/Or thinking and need to find yourself a better way to think. *What's the problem with Either/Or thinking?* It hems you in, limiting your options way too severely. Think of it: Suddenly, unwittingly, you've reduced a world of possibilities . . . to exactly two. Consider the following:

You're wondering whether to buy a new blender when the sales clerk cleverly says: "Would you like the blue one or the red one?" A moment ago you were entertaining a myriad of options—*Should I buy it? Not buy it? Wait till they have a sale? Find a better price on the Internet?*" Now, thanks to that sneaky salesperson, your options number exactly two:

Should I choose the RED one?
Or should I choose the BLUE one?

Derm Barrett, in his book *The Paradox Process,* warns (rightly so) that the "tyranny of 'or' " precludes the "genius of 'and.' " Consider the 1950s "battling twins" ad campaign for Certs. One twin says: "Certs is a breath mint." The other replies: "No, Certs is a candy mint." Then the announcer steps in: "Stop. You're both right: Certs is two. Two! Two mints in one!"

Today, automakers are combining solutions for another "and" alternative: hybrid cars that feature an electric motor AND a gasoline engine, offering, if you will, the "best of both worlds." (Toyota's two. Two! Two cars in one!)

Consider the classic dilemma: *Should I get a manual or an automatic?* Clearly, this is an Either/Or situation—*if you fail to question assumptions.* In fact, *Manual or automatic?* has an excellent AND solution: a tiptronic transmission that allows you to choose—as you drive—"manual" or "automatic," allowing you to have, in effect, an automatic transmission AND a manual transmission.

Finally, here's a legitimate Either/Or choice: *Should I buy a new car or a used car?* If you're looking to buy a car, there are no other alternatives: *Either I get a new car or I get a used one.*

But is that really so?

In fact, if you *question your assumptions* you may discover an "and" solution: a certified preowned car, combining the value of a used car AND the benefit of a manufacturer's guarantee.

Choosers beware:

When facing what appears to be an "Either/Or" situation, look to combine solutions with the "genius" of AND.

For example . . .

Country or Pop?

Some fans have trouble deciding whether Shania Twain is a country singer or a pop performer. To address that Either/Or head on, in 2002 Shania released a *double* CD (*UP!*): One disc has country arrangements of 19 new songs; the other disc has pop arrangements of the very same songs. The result? *UP!* ranked number eight among the top selling albums of the year, with worldwide sales of NINE MILLION units. (Looks like the "twains" have met after all—and with success.)

Comedy or Tragedy?

Woody Allen's film, *Melinda and Melinda* (2005), presents its own "and" solution: the story of Melinda's life from two different perspectives: Story A (the "tragedy" of Melinda) and Story B (the "comedy" of Melinda).

Corporate Profit or Social Responsibility?

Is the sole purpose of a corporation to make its stockholders happy, even at the expense of social considerations? Robert S. MacNamara, interviewed in *The Fog of War* (2004), insists: "Corporate executives must recognize there is no contradiction between a soft heart and a strong head. Of course, they have responsibilities to stockholders, but they also have responsibilities to their employees, their customers, and to society as a whole."

But wait, there's more . . .

Early in the movie *A Beautiful Mind* (2001), mathematician John Nash (Russell Crowe) starts teaching a class in a room that's too darn hot. Hoping for relief, he opens a window. Unfortunately, this lets in the sound of workers jackhammering below. Back down goes the window, until a young student (Jennifer Connelly) gets up and reopens the window. Crowe objects, insisting he'd rather have the heat than the noise. ("So I can hear myself think.") For a moment, they're at loggerheads. Then Connelly uses her feminine charm—and her brains: Leaning out the window, she asks the workers below if they wouldn't mind working somewhere else for the next forty minutes. In other words: Connelly breaks out of a no-win Either/Or stalemate (closed and hot or open and noisy) by proposing a THIRD—and winning!—solution: Cool AND quiet. (In fact, the workers readily agree to her proposal and Crowe is smitten, both by her good looks AND her savvy.)

That said, it's time to add another "and" to our "Either/Or" mantra:

When facing what appears to be an "Either/Or" situation, look to *combine* solutions with the "genius" of AND. (And keep looking for MORE solutions!)

Consider, for example . . .

ETHICS AND THE TRAP OF "EITHER-OR"

In seminars on leadership and decision making, there's a popular precursor to TV's *Survivor*—that old chestnut, the "lifeboat exercise." (If you know it, stick with me. The solution will surprise you.) In the exercise, students are asked to imagine that a ship is sinking and that the lifeboat isn't big enough to accommodate all the survivors. Heavy winds and waves threaten to sink the lifeboat as well. Given thumbnail descriptions of the motley crew, students are asked: "Which survivors should be thrown overboard?" *The mentally disturbed one-armed man who carries government secrets in his head? Or the prostitute who's also an excellent nurse?* And so on.

Chances are you'll never find yourself in quite the same situation. But the exercise serves as a great teaching example. In fact, the most ethical decision can only be discovered if you're daring enough to question assumptions.

TRUE STORY

In 1943, the SS *Deer Lodge* was torpedoed by a German U-boat. Seas were rough and winds were heavy. Men were sick, injured, and the too-small lifeboat was in danger of sinking. With little discussion and no debate, here's what they did: *While the stronger men stayed on board to bail, others took turns going over the side, hanging on to the gunwales as their only support. In the end, every crewman was saved.*

What the crewmen decided—right from the start!—was the opposite of our classroom assumption. Instead of thinking, SOMEONE has to go . . . their assumption was NO ONE has to go!

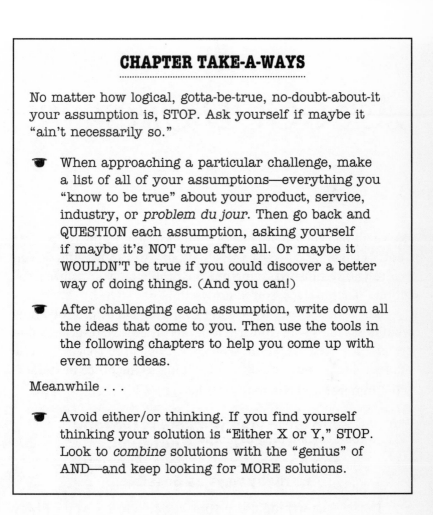

CHAPTER TAKE-A-WAYS

No matter how logical, gotta-be-true, no-doubt-about-it your assumption is, STOP. Ask yourself if maybe it "ain't necessarily so."

- When approaching a particular challenge, make a list of all of your assumptions—everything you "know to be true" about your product, service, industry, or *problem du jour*. Then go back and QUESTION each assumption, asking yourself if maybe it's NOT true after all. Or maybe it WOULDN'T be true if you could discover a better way of doing things. (And you can!)
- After challenging each assumption, write down all the ideas that come to you. Then use the tools in the following chapters to help you come up with even more ideas.

Meanwhile . . .

- Avoid either/or thinking. If you find yourself thinking your solution is "Either X or Y," STOP. Look to *combine* solutions with the "genius" of AND—and keep looking for MORE solutions.

8

Ask GOOD Questions

We've all had the experience of going for help to the office next door. "Listen, Jack. Here's the situation." And sometimes—even before you've finished laying out the problem—you realize a solution. "Thanks, Jack, solved it myself!"

The lesson? Never try to solve your problem before you know what it is. That's why your trip to Jack's office was so successful—because it forced you to present your problem in a clear, precise manner. Since you can't always be going to the office next door, remember to follow this simple rule:

Write down your problem in the form of a clear, precise question. And be sure to POSE that question as many ways as possible.

In fact, just writing down your question brings you halfway to the answer. As Edwin Land, creator of the Polaroid Land camera believed: "If you are able to state a problem—any problem—and if it is important enough, then the problem can be solved." But don't stop there; because the more ways you pose your question, the better your odds of finding the right question—and the right answers.

For example, imagine that as the manager of an office building, you're getting a growing number of complaints from the building's tenants about how long they have to wait before an elevator arrives. You decide to call in a consultant to advise you.

Question: What type of consultant do you hire?

Naturally enough, most people answer, "An elevator consultant." And that's a fair answer. But it's certainly not the only answer. First, let's go back a bit and see if you took the time to follow the advice on the previous page. Namely:

Write down your problem in the form of a clear, precise question. And be sure to POSE that question as many ways as possible.

Before you start asking "What kind of consultant do I hire?" how about asking "What kind of problem do I have?" Is it a "mechanical" problem?

"How do I speed up the elevators?"

Or is it a "people" problem?

"How do I get these people to STOP COMPLAINING!"?

Naturally, each of these questions will result in a very different kind of answer: the difference, perhaps, between spending hundreds of thousands of dollars to upgrade the system, or just what it costs to buy a bunch of mirrors and place them by the elevators—so people can spend their time primping and preening instead of being focused on how long their elevator is taking. Or you could do both—upgrade the elevators *and* put up mirrors. Regardless, the lesson is clear (and worth repeating):

The more ways you POSE your question the better your odds of finding the right QUESTION– and the right ANSWERS.

A similar solution was devised after callers to a business kept complaining about how many RINGS it took for someone to answer their call. *The solution?* Instead of hiring more people, they increased the LENGTH of each ring—so callers heard just two or three rings instead of four or five. And just like that . . . people stopped complaining.

Picture This: A man facing a firing squad, twenty rifles aimed at his heart. Afraid of loud noises, he sticks his fingers in his ears.

Now Picture This: A woman driving a late model Mercedes. Smoking a cigarette, she's careful to blow the smoke out the window. *Takes a drag, EXHALES out the window. Takes a drag, EXHALES out the window.*

What do both scenarios have in common? They're both examples of people who've managed to solve a problem. Only problem is, they've both solved the WRONG problem.

Consider, for example, the growing trend among states and many countries to ban the use of handheld cell phones while driving—despite a body of research (both from Canada and the United States) demonstrating that handheld phones are NOT the problem per se. At the University of Utah, for example, David Strayer, Ph.D., compared the effect of handheld vs. hands-free phones. His conclusion, as he told *Consumer Reports,* is that there is "no safety advantage for using a hands-free vs. a hand-held phone. It's conversation that drives this effect. When you're talking, you're impaired." Yet legislators—failing to QUESTION THEIR ASSUMPTIONS—continue to press for bans on handheld phones only.

Lesson learned? (One more time, for emphasis.)

Remember to pose your question AS MANY WAYS AS POSSIBLE *(Are handheld phones the problem? Or is the problem talking on ANY cell phone?)*. By posing your question DIFFERENT WAYS not only will you be CHALLENGING YOUR ASSUMPTIONS, you'll be INCREASING YOUR CHANCES of solving the RIGHT problem in the first place.

My mechanic told me, "I couldn't fix your brakes so I made the horn louder."

—Stephen Wright

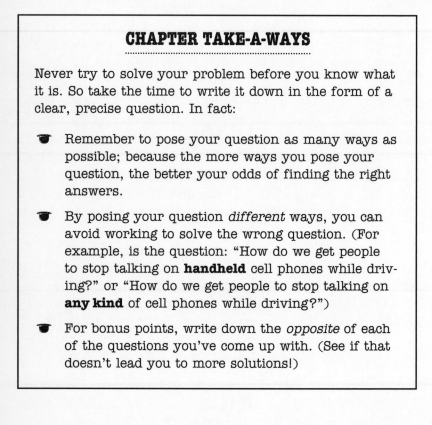

CHAPTER TAKE-A-WAYS

Never try to solve your problem before you know what it is. So take the time to write it down in the form of a clear, precise question. In fact:

- Remember to pose your question as many ways as possible; because the more ways you pose your question, the better your odds of finding the right answers.
- By posing your question *different* ways, you can avoid working to solve the wrong question. (For example, is the question: "How do we get people to stop talking on **handheld** cell phones while driving?" or "How do we get people to stop talking on **any kind** of cell phones while driving?")
- For bonus points, write down the *opposite* of each of the questions you've come up with. (See if that doesn't lead you to more solutions!)

9

Take an "Opposites" Approach

A sure-fire way to test your assumptions is to ask yourself, "What's the 'opposite' of my question?" Not only will it force you to think in new, unexpected ways, it often leads to one or more outstanding solutions.

The original "opposites" thinker was Tom Sawyer. When faced with the question:

How am I going to do all this work?

Tom turned the problem on its head, coming up with the provocative "opposite":

How are <u>you</u> going to do all this <u>fun</u>?

By asking the "opposite" of his question, Tom challenged his assumption and discovered a winning solution: no more work for Tom and lots more "fun" for his unsuspecting friends.

Question: Will every question you face have an absolute "opposite" that instantly wins the day? Hardly. You'll discover that a particular question may reveal any number of "opposites"—and not all of them will lead you to a wise and wonderful solution. Suppose you're a Family Court Judge searching for a solution to truancy. Starting with the question:

How do I get truant kids to go to school?

The opposites approach calls for creating as many variations or "opposites" as you can:

How do I get truant kids to <u>not</u> go to school?
How do I get truant <u>adults</u> to go to school?
How do <u>you</u> get truant kids to go to school?
How do <u>you</u> get truant kids to not go to school?
(And so on.)

Take a moment now to study the "opposites" above. Do any of them create a "Yes, that's it!" visceral response? If not, don't despair. While many—or even ALL—of your "opposites" may seem to lead you nowhere but down a dead-end street, usually, with a bit of mental prowess, you can work your "opposites" until, with one or more of them, sense—and solution—finally appear. In fact, here's a real-life solution that seems to have sprung from the second "opposite" on our list:

How do I get truant <u>adults</u> to go to school?

In 2002, Orange County Judge Robert Hutson debuted a new solution for combating truancy when he ordered the father of a nine-year-old to attend his son's fourth-grade classes at least once a month. *There's a solution that might just do the trick!* Simple. Easy. And economical.

Remember: Not every "opposite" will instantly lead you to a "Eureka!" response. It's a numbers game—as dependant on the number of "opposites" you're willing to entertain as on your ability to "work" the process. Consider, for example, the fifth grade teacher who used to loan out her pencils to unprepared students but seldom got them back. First she asked:

How do I get them to return my stuff?

Then she turned the question upside down, asking, instead:

How do <u>they</u> get <u>me</u> to return <u>their</u> stuff?

Again, it may have taken her a bit of head scratching to figure out what-the-heck that question could mean, but—sure enough—she discovered her solution: Now, whenever her students borrow one of her pencils, she makes sure they leave her one of their shoes.

"You want your <u>shoe</u> back?
I want my <u>pencil</u> back!"

Where else can the "opposites" approach do its magic? *Anywhere at all.*

Inventing

In creating the Palm Pilot, Jeff Hawkins started out trying to write software for a small handheld device that was sophisticated enough to recognize millions of different handwriting styles asking himself.

How do I teach this device lots of different handwriting styles?

Pretty soon, however, he found himself posing an opposite question:

How do I teach the users of this device one handwriting style?

The result? Graffiti. (And lots and lots of money.)

Teaching

Cyberspace makes cheating on term papers easier than ever. Years ago, you had to write a check, mail it off to a term paper company, then wait to get your paper. Now you can go to sites like www.schoolsucks.com and instantly download any paper you want. To combat the trend, a group of professors banded together and created a database of papers and a search engine to look for plagiarized papers—their way of fighting fire with fire. There is, however, a very "opposite" point of view.

Donald L. McCabe, a national plagiarism expert at Rutgers University says that rather than catching students AFTER the fact, ". . . more efforts need to go into teaching students not to cheat" in the first place. So instead of asking:

How do we catch them after they've cheated?

McCabe says we should be asking:

How do we catch them before they've cheated?

McCabe's solution? Teach them *ethics.*

While searching for just the right grade school for our son, my wife and I asked the principal of one of the schools a raft of questions. One question, "What do you do about bullying?," was met with the instant reply: "We teach citizenship." *Catching the problem BEFORE it's a problem.*

Yet another "opposites" approach is suggested by Wolfram Latsch, professor of economics at Northwestern University, who writes: "If you look at the many commercial term paper sites on the Internet, you will find that there are large numbers of papers for only a small number of topics. [The problem is that] the same . . . term paper topics are assigned again and again. . . . If professors were more creative and less repetitive in their teaching, [the] market for one-size-fits-all term papers would not work as well."

In other words: It's not just a student problem, it's also a TEACHER problem.

Selling Pizza

When Gino Pala managed his family's café in Wilmington, Delaware, he placed a one-of-a-kind sign out front: "World's Worst Pizza." And it worked! Passersby appreciated the humor and dared to take a chance. Besides, only someone with really *great* pizza can afford to proclaim it the "worst" in the world.

My own son, age seven at the time, took a similar approach while at a tradeshow booth for *Shake It!* Books: "You don't want these books," he called out. "They're boring and overpriced." And just like that . . . he made a $100 sale.

Dealing with Returns

In Beverly Hills, a man visited high-end clothier Malcolm Levene and bought a four-thousand-dollar overcoat. What's the problem, you ask? Next day, the man's wife sent her husband back to return it. Not only did Levene persuade the man to keep the coat, he took the opportunity to sell him two suits—for an additional sale of two thousand dollars.

Levene's philosophy? "A return is not a return—it's an opportunity."

Let the "opposites" approach lead you to FUN as well.

For example, here's how to turn your frustration with telemarketers into an opportunity for FUN. Instead of asking:

How do I get telemarketers to stop annoying me?

Let's explore the more provocative question:

How do I start annoying them?

The next time a telemarketer calls, try some of these:

- "Let me sell *you* something. My house is for sale. Like to buy it?"
- "You sound cute. Tell me what you look like and don't leave *anything* out!"
- "The person you're calling for is in Zanzibar and won't be back for a couple of years. Would you like me to take a message?"

True Story

The Marx Brothers—stationed just outside the office of Irving Thalberg, head of production for MGM—were waiting for their meeting with the studio Big Shot. But as Hollywood Big Shots are wont to do, Thalberg kept them waiting. And waiting. And waiting some more. Finally, they figured: *If we're not getting into his office, he's not getting OUT!* So they grabbed some furniture and filing cabinets, stacked them up against his door, and calmly took off for a day at the races.

Chair Deprived

What's the first thing everyone does just before a meeting? *Sit down.* But what if we took an "opposites" approach? What if—instead of saying, "As soon as everyone gets seated we can get started"—we said, "As soon as we get finished, everyone can get seated?" What would happen if everyone had to STAND UP—and *keep* standing up—until the meeting was over? People would stay on topic and meetings would be shorter. Or how about a meeting out in the hall? No sitting. No leaning on the wall. Just staying on topic and on schedule.

Store Deprived

When Aaron Montgomery Ward launched his mail order empire—the Montgomery Ward catalog—he was following good instincts—and an "opposite" approach: If customers can't come to my store, he reasoned, I'll bring the store to them! (For a 20th-century update, consider online shopping. Same concept, different "delivery" system.)

Beach Deprived

In 2002, Paris Mayor Bertrand Delanoë spoke with an elderly woman who complained she couldn't afford to get away to the beach in the summer. The Mayor's solution? Bring *le plage*—the beach—to the center of Paris, for all those who could not get away themselves. His idea was met with cheers—and jeers. At a cost of $1.7 million dollars, many argued the money could be spent for more important things. But Delanoë pressed on, bringing in 1,000 tons of sand, potted palm trees in large wooden planters, and 150 lounge chairs and umbrellas, planting it all by the banks of the Seine. The result? An instant success with tourists and locals alike.

In fact, the event was so successful that the makeshift seaside resort has become an annual affair. One year later, in 2003, the sand order tripled to 3,000 tons, a third beachhead was installed, and chairs and umbrellas doubled to 300, along with 80 palm trees in large wooden planters. While the city's contribution remained the same, additional funding of nearly $1 million came from 15 selectively chosen sponsorship partners, from the state electricity company providing solar-paneled electricity to illuminate the areas at night, to Le Livre de Poche creating a lending library of paperbacks in different languages.

Meanwhile, other towns have rushed to imitate the event—including Budapest Plage, Berlin Plage, and Brussels Plage. If Mohammed can't go to the beach . . . let the beach come to Mohammed!

THE FRENCH FOR AMERICANS CLUB

Traveling through France just after college, I was determined to not be perceived as one more "stupid American." My solution? Dive in with my best high school French (a B+ on the best of days) and—if necessary—resort to my well-practiced plea for mercy: *Pardonnez-moi, je suis un Américain très stupide.* (Pardon me, I'm a very stupid American.)

1. It let them know I *knew* what they were thinking.
2. It suggested I wasn't so stupid after all.
3. It made them laugh, a good thing in any language.

THE BOOKS FOR CROOKS CLUB

One day, I received a fan letter about one of my books (*If You Can Talk, You Can Write*) from a convicted car thief, Dave, currently an inmate in a Kentucky prison. I immediately wrote back, enclosing Volume II (*If You're Writing, Let's Talk*) and feeling confident Dave would have the time to read it. A week later, my parcel was returned, stickered: REFUSED. Confused (and refused) I called up the prison to find out what the problem was. Turns out that inmates—after fourteen days of being there—may not receive packages of any kind. Whatever "extras" they'd like—like an undershirt or a candy bar—must be purchased at the prison commissary.

At first I was stumped. (That's where you start.)

How can I get this book to Dave?

That was my question—or at least the first way I posed my question. Soon, I posed my problem in an "opposite" way:

How can Dave get to this book?

The solution? Donate my book to the prison library and send Dave a letter telling him it's there. So that's what I did, making Dave and his fellow inmates "charter members" of my Books for Crooks Club.

HOW TO NOT FILTER OUT WEB SITES

Most web filters act to "filter out" objectionable content. But they all have their drawbacks: They filter too much, not enough, or—by making their own "to be filtered or not" decisions—can sometimes leave Mom and Dad wishing they had more parental control.

Taking an "OPPOSITES" approach is KidsDesk. Instead of asking:

How do we keep the bad stuff away?

KidsDesk asks:

How do we let the good stuff come in?

The solution? Mom and Dad hand pick which sites they find suitable for their kids to visit. Like to visit a site that's not on Mom and Dad's approved list? *Can't go.* Like to search their hard drive? *Can't go there, either.* "Think of it," wrote an amazon.com reviewer, "as a really cool prison."

True, KidsDesk works best with younger children who are more likely to be satisfied with a smaller list of places they can visit. But the lesson is clear: By taking an "opposites" approach, KidsDesk provides an elegant alternative.

HOW TO CURE CANCER? DON'T

In a scathing indictment of the American Cancer Society and the National Cancer Institute, Drs. Samuel S. Epstein and Quentin D. Young present an "opposites" approach to battling cancer. In an Op Ed piece for the *Los Angeles Times*, they write: "[T]he cancer establishment's focus remains fixated on damage control—screening, diagnosis, treatment, and related basic research—rather than on preventing cancer in the first place. The things on which we're spending money are important and fully deserve substantial funding. But much less spending on cures would be needed if more cancers were prevented. . . . [F]ar too little is being spent on research into avoidable causes of cancer, including environmental contaminants of air, water, soil, the workplace, and food." They conclude: "The war on cancer is certainly winnable. But we've spent many years and billions of dollars focusing on cures. Focusing on prevention instead would not only save lives: It would save dollars."

In other words, instead of asking . . .

How do we CURE cancer?

Epstein and Young posit an "opposite" question:

How do we PREVENT cancer?

Credentials: Dr. Samuel S. Epstein is chairman of the Cancer Prevention Coalition and professor emeritus at the University of Illinois at Chicago School of Public Health. Dr. Quentin D. Young is chairman of the Health and Medicine Policy Research Group, Chicago, and former president of the American Public Health Association.

HOW TO DISCOURAGE BOOK BUYERS FROM BUYING

Daniel Handler, writing under the name Lemony Snicket, took an "opposites" approach in creating the incredibly popular children's book series, "A Series of Unfortunate Events" (later made into a film starring Jim Carrey). On the back of each book he warns potential readers they may prefer to read something else. As he writes about the first book in the series:

> Dear Reader,
>
> I'm sorry to say that the book you are holding in your hands is extremely unpleasant. It tells an unhappy tale about three very unlucky children. Even though they are charming and clever, the Baudelaire siblings lead lives filled with misery and woe. From the very first page of this book when the children are at the beach and receive terrible news,

continuing on through the entire story, disaster lurks at their heels. One might say they are magnets for misfortune.

In this short book alone, the three youngsters encounter a greedy and repulsive villain, itchy clothing, a disastrous fire, a plot to steal their fortune, and cold porridge for breakfast.

It is my sad duty to write down these unpleasant tales, but there is nothing stopping you from putting this book down at once and reading something happy, if you prefer that sort of thing.

With all due respect,

Lemony Snicket

Working to protect the identity of his pseudonym, Snicket's photograph appears in the back of each book—photographed each time from *behind* (yet another "opposites" solution). In one thumbnail biographical paragraph he writes that "Lemony Snicket is the author of quite a few books, all dreadful," in another that "Lemony Snicket was born before you were and is likely to die before you as well."

Meanwhile, Handler "challenges assumptions" by dedicating each book (more than ten so far) to the very same person, Beatrice, with warm, loving thoughts like: "To Beatrice—darling, dearest, dead." and "For Beatrice—when we were together I felt breathless. Now, you are."

Bottom line? Here's an "opposites approach" yielding work that is unfortunate, unpleasant, and undeniably successful.

HOW TO GET A CROWD FOR SQUASH

How do you get Americans interested in watching a game of *squash*? Hold the Bear Stearns Tournament of Champions INSIDE New York City's Grand Central Station. That's what they did in 2004, placing the court's front glass wall in easy view of anyone passing through the station's Vanderbilt Hall. The goal? That giving a "free peek" to the 120,000 people who pass by each of the eight tournament days will help create greater interest in the sport. *If the public will not come to the game, then the game will come to the public.*

What do you do about gun control? NOTHING

"You don't need no gun control," says Chris Rock. "You know what [we] need? We need some *bullet* control. . . . I think all bullets should cost five thousand dollars. Five thousand dollars for a bullet. You know why? 'Cause if a bullet costs five thousand dollars there'll be no more innocent bystanders. . . . People would *think* before they killed somebody if a bullet cost five thousand dollars. 'Man, I would blow your . . . head off—if I could afford it.' "

HOW TO SOLVE THE HEALTH-CARE PROBLEM

Mark Twain famously quipped, "Everyone talks about the weather but no one does anything about it." Today, you're just as likely to hear people talking—and complaining—about the rising cost of health care. Instead of just complaining—"Don't find a fault," said Henry Ford, "find a remedy." Let's see what happens when we state our problem (as suggested earlier) in the form of one or more questions, then look for the "opposite" of those questions. For example:

How can we spend less on disease?

Becomes:

How can we spend more on health?

And:

How can we lower the cost of disease?

Becomes:

How can we raise the benefit of health?

Looking at the first "opposite" question—"How can we spend more on health?"—the answer seems apparent: preventive measures like eating right, quitting smoking, and exercising regularly. For example, there are employers that have on-site health facilities or fitness classes, and others that pay for a portion of employee's health care costs. Some even reward employees with bonuses for meeting fitness goals. Better food in the company cafeteria is also smart business. The concept is clear: *The more we pay for generating good heath, the less we'll pay in medical costs. And there will be a net savings overall.*

Now before we start a victory lap or toast ourselves with a carrot juice, let's return to our second original question—"How can we lower the cost of disease?"—and ask it not in an "opposites" way, but just in a *slightly different* way. For example:
How can we lower the cost of disease for our *future* employees?

That's interesting. What if a company divided its workers into two groups: Current Employees and Future Employees? Your current employees are what you've already got, and as a leader (in this case, a *health* leader) you're job is to do the best with what you've got. In terms of *future employees,* however, what if you decided to "pick and choose" with an eye toward future health care costs? To put that in plain English: What if you simply refused to hire smokers and overweight applicants as a way to reduce future heath care costs?

At the time of this writing (2005) twenty-eight states and the District of Columbia have laws that protect workers from discrimination because of smoking. That leaves twenty-two states (44 percent of the country) where, from an employer's perspective, it's still open season on smokers. Their rationale? People who smoke have more heath problems, and more health care costs, than people who don't. (Same goes for overweight people.) So one way for an employer to save money is simply to *avoid* hiring smokers and overweight candidates. Simple. Neat. And entirely legal in twenty-two states. It may seem cruel. It may seem heartless. And it may seem perfectly reasonable.

Nick Connon, a labor attorney and cofounder of Connon & Wood, opines: "An employer can refuse to hire anyone for any reason as long as it is not an unlawful reason. Don't like redheads or people with long hair? Don't hire them. In fact, if policies against hiring smokers or overweight people cause people to stop smoking or get on the treadmill in order to get a job, it could be seen as a good thing."

Now let's go back to that first question—"How can we lower the cost of disease?"—and apply it to Current Employees only. Remember where I suggested that your current employees were a given, so to speak? And that it was your job "to do the best with what you've got"? One assumption we *failed to challenge* was that you had to "do the best" with those workers you already have. What if we *challenged that assumption*? What if we said, instead: *Those workers we currently have who are already smokers, we'll fire them for smoking.*

I know. I know. It sounds preposterous. Yet one company, Weyco Inc., an Illinois-based *medical benefits* administrator did just that on January 1, 2005. "We told them they had a choice,"

Weyco Chief Financial Officer Gary Climes told the *Chicago Tribune,* either kick the habit with the help of company-provided smoking cessation classes and support groups or get kicked out of your job. (While about twenty of the company's workers wound up quitting, four did not.) "We're not saying you can't smoke in your home," said Climes. "We just say you can't smoke and work here."

KIDS AND OPPOSITES

In the late 1990s, Owens Corning asked, *What's the best way to educate adults about conserving energy?* Their solution? *Educate kids and let* them *hound their parents.* The company distributed to schools 10,000 educational kits ("Saving Energy Starts With Me") containing material for students and a teacher's guide for a three-day course. In addition, nearly 1,000 kids joined in an essay-writing contest, "Why Energy Savings Starts With Me." The result? The campaign earned 270 media placements and more than a quarter million children and parents took a long hard look at the energy efficiency of their homes. And it all started by asking an "opposites" question.

About the same time, in 1997, I took a similar approach. Instead of asking, *What can adults teach me about parenting,* I went straight to the rank and file, asking kids (ages six to twelve): "If you could tell someone how to be the perfect parent, what would you tell them?" The result of my "opposites" research was the best-selling book, *Always Kiss Me Good Night: Instructions on Raising the Perfect Parent by 147 Kids Who Know* (1993), created by J. S. Salt (aka Joel Saltzman). I then took a similar "opposites" approach to create two more best sellers—*How to Be The Almost Perfect Husband: By Wives Who Know* (2000) and *How to Be The Almost Perfect Wife: By Husbands Who Know* (2000).

A bit self-promotional, you say? As Bill Clinton remarked in his autobiography, "If you don't toot your own horn, no one else will." (Which I was surprised to read because I thought someone else had.)

TRUE STORY

Wynton Marsalis and his jazz band were coming to town and I was determined to have my son meet him. My concern, though, was that if we lined up with everyone else after the show, we might not be successful. So we did the opposite—showed up two hours *early* and met the stage manager, Maurice, outside at the stage door. Maurice put us on the guest list and promised we'd be able to meet and talk with Wynton after the show. ("And if anyone gives you trouble, you just tell 'em to go get me.") After the show, as expected, there was a large crowd hoping to meet Wynton. Yet my son and I breezed right in—first class all the way. The people in line stared at us, wondering, *What makes them so special?* or *Gee, they must they know Wynton!* What made us so "special" was that we had tried an "opposites" approach—trying to meet the star *before* the show instead of *after*.

The moment Wynton saw us he called out to my son, "I like you already. Look at that smile!" Wynton put his arm around him, posed for photos, and gave my son a moment he'll remember for the rest of his life. "Dad, I met a real life hero!"

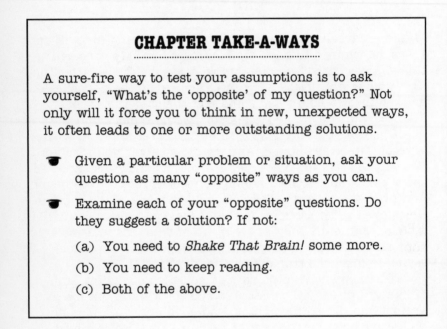

CHAPTER TAKE-A-WAYS

A sure-fire way to test your assumptions is to ask yourself, "What's the 'opposite' of my question?" Not only will it force you to think in new, unexpected ways, it often leads to one or more outstanding solutions.

- Given a particular problem or situation, ask your question as many "opposite" ways as you can.
- Examine each of your "opposite" questions. Do they suggest a solution? If not:

  (a) You need to *Shake That Brain!* some more.

  (b) You need to keep reading.

  (c) Both of the above.

10

Never Take NO for an ANSWER

Picture This: As the result of your "opposites" thinking—or maybe just out of the blue—you get an idea. It's a great idea. A REALLY great idea. Then you think about it a bit and pretty soon—maybe just a few seconds later—you're thinking, *I was wrong; it's not a good idea at all. After all, if it's my idea, how good could it possibly be!?* (Or perhaps your "then again" reaction is more like: *But am I prepared to deal with all the* resistance *I'm sure to encounter?*)

Now Picture This: You get past Hurdle One (above) and summon the courage to present your idea to someone other than yourself; someone who has no problem at all telling you why your brainchild is boneheaded or just won't work.

Whether you're your own naysayer, or someone else wields the axe, the real problem is this: It's hard to be a good predictor—at least at first—of whether something is a GOOD idea or a BAD idea. That's why it's a BAD idea to say it's a bad idea—because it could turn out to be a very GOOD idea.

The history of new ideas, it could be argued, is the history of rejections overcome. As Carl R. Rogers explained: "The very essence of the creative is its novelty, and hence we have no standard by which to judge it."

Whether it's your idea or someone else's, instead of saying, "That's not it!" learn to say, "That *could* be it." In other words: **Just say YES** and see where it takes you.

TRUE STORY

In the 1930s and 40s, when Chuck Jones and his cohorts at Warner Bros. were creating their famous Looney Tunes cartoons (featuring Bugs Bunny, Daffy Duck, Porky Pig, etc.), they took a far more enlightened approach to fostering new ideas. At regular meetings, called "Big Yes" sessions, the rule was that every story idea or gag that was pitched could only be greeted with a Yes. As Jones explained, "For two hours . . . you could only contribute to the idea, and that meant that all negatives were out." People were free to offer changes or modifications but they had to focus on the positive.

In the 1950s, at The Second City improvisational theater in Chicago, cofounder Del Close created the cardinal rule of improvisation, "Yes, and______," meaning that each performer must "agree with any premise, no matter how absurd, and then follow and amplify it, working with fellow players who will 'yes, and' any idea of yours."

Remember Dahl's idea for a pet rock and his buddies who "started to riff with [his] off-the-wall idea," coming up with "all the things it was good for"? What they were doing was following Close's dictum to a tee—"agree with any premise, no matter how absurd, and then follow and amplify it."

Now. Imagine you're the head of a Hollywood studio when an animator pitches you on the idea of "a talking yellow sponge named Bob." Can you honestly say your knee-jerk reaction would have been: "Yes, and I think we should spend lots and lots of money to produce your series, SpongeBob SquarePants!"?

POP QUIZ: GOOD IDEA OR BAD IDEA?

Imagine you're in charge of a hypothetical Suggestion Box. Review the following ideas and judge for yourself: "Good Idea?" Or "Bad Idea?" Once you've made your decisions, see how you rate on the Idea Prognosticator Scale—a pseudoscientific measurement of your ability to sniff out the good ideas and toss out the bad ones. (Remember: Keep your eye on your own paper and do not skip ahead to the Answers section before responding to each of the following ten suggestions.)

Suggestion 1: A concrete boat.

___ Good idea

___ Bad idea

Suggestion 2: Cat litter for dogs.

___ Good idea

___ Bad idea

Suggestion 3: A seeing eye pony.

___ Good idea

___ Bad idea

Suggestion 4: Playboy magazine on radio.

___ **Good idea**

___ **Bad idea**

Suggestion 5: A sex museum.

___ **Good idea**

___ **Bad idea**

Suggestion 6: Shopping for a jury at Wal-Mart.

___ **Good idea**

___ **Bad idea**

Suggestion 7: Civility school for lawyers.

___ **Good idea**

___ **Bad idea**

Suggestion 8: Teach AP calculus to remedial-math high school students.

___ **Good idea**

___ **Bad idea**

Suggestion 9: A parachute for an airplane—not for the passengers, for the *airplane*.

___ **Good idea**

___ **Bad idea**

Suggestion 10: When you have a disagreement with your spouse shout, "Shut up!"

___ **Good idea**

___ **Bad idea**

___ **Quick, run for cover!**

Answer Key

The best response for each of these suggestions is ***"Good idea!"*** To learn more, read on.

Suggestion 1: A concrete boat.

Good idea! Since 1985, the American Society of Civil Engineers has held the National Concrete Canoe Competition. The contestants? Engineering school students who compete over a 200-meter course. What makes 'em float? Good hull design and innovative concrete mixtures that need to contain at least 75 percent concrete.

Suggestion 2: Cat litter for dogs.

Good idea! Currently being marketed is Purina's *secondnature,* a "Litter & Housetraining System"—for dogs.

Suggestion 3: A seeing eye pony.

Good idea! And one that's in use. Miniature ponies weigh about 50 pounds and live a lot longer than dogs, about 35 to 40 years. In fact, in a worldwide poll, 27 percent of those asked said they would prefer a guide PONY if they required a guide animal. (Don't believe it? Visit: www.guidehorse.com)

Suggestion 4: Playboy on radio.

Good idea! While the idea of Playboy-without-pictures may at first sound absurd—like "a driver's manual in Braille," wrote one reviewer—it's been broadcast as a paid, premium service on XM Satellite Radio since 2002, promising its listeners: "the latest news from the sensual world . . . stories from the world of sex . . . Judge Julie's Sex Court . . . sizzling erotic fiction . . . and personal advice . . . from *The Playboy Advisor.*"

Suggestion 5: A sex museum.

Good idea! In 2002, the Museum of Sex (MOSEX) opened on New York City's Fifth Avenue with a mission—"to preserve and present the history, evolution, and cultural significance of human sexuality." In its first six weeks the museum attracted more than 15,000 visitors. Currently, the museum attracts more than 90,000 visitors a year.

Suggestion 6: Shopping for juries at Wal-Mart.

Good idea! Need some last minute jurors? Recently, judges have been sending deputies out to recruit jurors at local Wal-Mart and grocery stores. It's really quite simple: You're approached by a policeman who explains you have two choices: Show up for jury duty—immediately—or be held in contempt of court. It may sound *unusual* but it's legal—and effective.

Suggestion 7: Civility school for lawyers.

Good idea! Since 2004, lawyers in South Carolina have been required to take a one-hour civility class and to retake their oath, including the promise: "To opposing parties and their counsel, I pledge fairness, integrity, and civility, not only in court, but also in all written and oral communications." Apparently, things were getting out of hand. One prominent family lawyer got in trouble for "insulting, threatening, and demeaning" witnesses during depositions. Reportedly, this same lawyer said to one witness, "You are a mean-spirited, vicious witch and I don't like your face and I don't like your voice." Civics class for lawyers? *Great idea!*

Suggestion 8: Calculus for remedial math students.

Good idea! In the movie *Stand and Deliver* (1987), teacher Jaime Escalante (Edward James Olmos) takes a group of rebellious remedial math students and inspires them to take Advanced Placement Calculus and pass a state exam to prove their success. His fellow faculty think he's nuts, but Escalante won't hear of it, insisting: "Students will rise to the level of expectation." And they do. All eighteen students who take the AP test wind up passing. But the testing board is suspicious, and insists the students take the test a second time. Once again, they all pass the test. A Hollywood fairy tale, you say? The movie is based on a true story, and the ending—eighteen out of eighteen passing, *twice*—is exactly what happened. (Historical footnote: In the years that followed, more and more "remedial" students took and passed the AP test.)

Suggestion 9: Parachutes for airplanes.

Good idea! Since the early 1980s, Ballistic Recovery Systems, based in Minnesota, has delivered more than 19,000 parachute systems to owners of smaller aircraft. Featuring parachutes "as big as a house," the BRS System is credited with saving the lives of 167 people worldwide. In fact, NASA has recently invested $670,000 with BRS in the hopes of designing "a new generation of emergency parachutes that would work on small jets and could be steered by pilots as they drift to the ground."

Suggestion 10: Telling your spouse to "Shut up!"

Great idea! When my wife and I were vacationing in northern England, we stopped at a bed and breakfast run by an older couple. As the wife was telling us about the local attractions, her husband made the near-fatal mistake of trying to get a word in edgewise—to which his wife responded, in a high-pitched, yet very proper sounding accent: "Oh, shut up!" (And he did.) Today, when my wife and I are having a disagreement—and just before it escalates into a full-fledged battle-royale—one or the other of us is often smart enough to call out, in a high-pitched mock British accent:

"Oh, shut up!"

Said with humor, affection and—an absolute must!—that "high-pitched mock British accent," it cuts the tension, gives us a giggle, and lets the other person know how *both* of us feel. (To hear "Oh, shut up!" in action, visit: http://www.shakethatbrain.com/sound-ohshutup.html.)

How can you tell if it's a "bad idea"?

Easy. All it takes is a knee-jerk "No way!" reflex—either from others ("Bob, that's a dumb idea") or from yourself ("Bob, that's a dumb idea"). Remember Victor Kiam in that TV commercial? ("I liked the Remington Razor so much I bought the company.") Years earlier, Kiam was offered the patent for Velcro for $25,000

What's required is courage—the ability to stand up and be counted, to say, "This is a great idea!"—despite all criticism and negativity.

but turned it down because he failed to see its potential. Today, Velcro is a wildly profitable MONEY MAKER—for someone else.

Velcro? *Bad idea!*

The movie "Star Wars"—initially rejected by 12 major studios? *Bad idea!*

America Online? *Bad idea!*—recognized as such in 1985 when an investment banker, approached for venture capital, responded: "It's a dog. You should take it out back and shoot it." (Fast forward to today and that "dog" may still live to have another day.)

How about a rock 'n roll song called, "I've Got You, Babe"? You'd have to hear it first? Cher did, the same night Sonny wrote it. As Cher tells it: "After Sonny played her 'I've Got You, Babe' she shrugged her shoulders and went to bed." Later that year, Sonny's less than stellar work went on to become their most popular hit.

Finally . . .

How about a book of parenting advice written by kids and presented in their own handwriting? Initially rejected by fourteen publishers, *Always Kiss Me Good Night: How to Be The Almost Perfect Parent by 147 Kids Who Know* was eventually purchased by Random House. Their only condition was that the creator of the

Ray and Stan BREAK the Mold

As Ray Charles recalled in his autobiography, *Brother Ray*: "When I mentioned to [Sam Clark, then president of ABC-Paramount Records] that I wanted to do an album of country music, he said, 'You've spent so much time building a career, doing a country album might lose some of your fans.' My response was that though I might lose some fans, if I play it right, I just might gain more than I lose."

Originally derided as "Ray's folly" by many in the industry, *Modern Sounds in Country and Western Music* turned out to be a "good idea" after all. Crossing over to the pop charts, it became the Number One album of 1962.

Likewise, when creator Stan Lee first pitched the idea of Spider Man, his boss also had misgivings: "Here I draw the line," Lee recalls him saying. "People HATE spiders. [Besides,] teenagers can only be side-kicks, not superheroes." But stubborn Stan refused to budge. Not only did Spider Man go on to become a legendary comic book hero, but forty years after that initial rejection the Spider Man movie grossed an astonishing $800 million just six months after its release. (Déjà vu Update: The studio's initial reaction to the idea of Tobey Maguire playing the lead? *Bad idea!*)

project include "at least 25 drawings from children." Afraid he'd get nothing but "smiling faces and rainbows" the author was convinced the drawings were a "Bad idea!" Nonetheless, he went along with the change. (1) He wanted the money, and (2) He was willing to entertain that even though HE thought it was a bad idea, he might just be wrong.

Published in 1997, *Always Kiss Me Good Night* has sold more than 150,000 copies to date and ranks among Random House's top ten gift books—in spite of fourteen rejection letters with comments like "gimmicky," "repetitive," and "sad and depressing." As for the addition of those drawings, it turned out—according to author J. S. Salt (aka Joel Saltzman)—not to be a "Good idea," but a "Great idea!" (For selections from the book—including some of those drawings—go to: http://www.shakethatbrain.com/stb-selections-01.html.)

In fact, what's very often deemed to be a *Bad idea!* by others is simply the FIRST VERSION or FIRST INCARNATION. Imagine showing someone an acorn and telling them your idea for an oak tree. Instead, they flicked it aside, saying *Bad idea!* Ideas—like tiny acorns—need time to grow and evolve.

You need vision ("It's a great idea!), persistence in the face of skepticism ("It's STILL a great idea!"), and the willingness to change or adapt along the way—either to gain support, improve your idea, or both.

In the case of *Always Kiss Me Good Night,* my first vision for the book was that I'd interview a bunch of kids, get their advice on how to be a good parent, and transcribe their words into a collection of one to two sentence bits of advice. That idea (Version I) was knee-jerk rejected by my agent ("*Not so hotsy-totsy*") and met with a shrug by my wife. Later, as I began to work on the idea—"despite all criticism and negativity"—I *modified* my idea by deciding to include the kids' own handwriting (Version II). And that idea, as you've already read, was *further* modified by the publisher, which (wisely, it turns out) mandated the inclusion of the children's drawings as well.

So what may have started out as an idea that was "*Not so hotsy-totsy,*" got changed, added to, and, over time, became much BETTER than my original idea. That's what happens sometimes:

**X becomes Y,
becomes "Why" didn't we
say Yes to X in the first place?**

TRUE STORY

In 1997, entrepreneur Reed Hastings had an idea. *Get people to rent DVDs over the Internet, then deliver them via the mail.* Today, with companies like Blockbuster and Wal-Mart doing just that, it seems like a pretty good idea. But in 1997, recalls Hastings, "People thought this idea was crazy—that consumers would rent movies through the mail."

Hastings' original idea, X, was to have consumers rent videos one-at-a-time and—just like Blockbuster did it at the time—charge them a late fee if the DVD was not returned on time. Sixteen months after launch, however, X became Y—a subscription service where users could keep movies for as long as they liked. Rent up to three movies at a time, keep them as long as you like, then return them in the preaddressed, prestamped envelopes whenever you're ready for more.

Again, the formula is simple:

**X becomes Y,
becomes "Why" didn't we
say Yes to X in the first place?**

And so, after watching Netflix for a number of years, big-league players like Blockbuster and Wal-Mart decided to follow the model, improve on it where they could, and join the bandwagon for what turned out to be a very "Good idea!" after all.

While Hastings can't deny feeling pressure from the competition—not to mention the not-so-far-in-the-distance threat of video-on-demand via the Web—he also feels a certain satisfaction for having been right after all—at least up till now. "To be doubted and be successful," he says, "is particularly satisfying."

"The really good idea," writes John Cleese, "is always traceable back quite a long way, often to a not very good idea which sparked off another idea that was only slightly better, which somebody else misunderstood in such a way that they then said something which was really rather interesting." And he wasn't far off the mark. Though it doesn't really require that initial idea being "misunderstood," it does require one or more "only slightly better" ideas along the way.

Consider the Mae West flotation vest—named after the buxom film star because it endowed the wearer with a similar figure. (A device, by the way, that Cleese would surely have fun with.) The original "not very good idea" was to fill the vest with duck feathers. But, as inventor Andrew Toti recalled, it made the vest "too bulky and heavy, so I switched to air"—an invention that proved to be "really rather interesting," and quite useful. Adopted by the War Department for World War II, the Mae West vest kept afloat thousands of downed Allied pilots.

Now let's go back in time a bit, to *before* Toti replaced his duck feathers with automatic carbon-dioxide inflation. Can you imagine *anyone* saying, "Duck feathers. What a great idea!" And yet . . . that's where Toti started.

As Henry Ford put it: "Failure is only the opportunity to begin again more intelligently." *Exactly!* The secret is you must begin. For unless you take that first "not very good idea" and move ahead with it, there is no chance whatsoever of seeing X become Y become *Why didn't we see what a great idea it was in the first place!?"*

Writer Henry Miller noted that "Writing, like life, is a voyage of discovery." Same goes for inventing . . . creating . . . or going from *any* X to *any* Y, no matter the topic or field of pursuit.

Of course, not every off-the-wall idea turns out to be a Good Idea. Many really are *Bad Ideas* headed for no good at all. (For example, a *python-filled* flotation device.) Still, the smart way to go is to follow a fundamental rule: Don't say *No!* to a new idea simply because it CHALLENGES common sense or some time-honored way of how things are done. After all, "Common sense," noted physicist Stephen Hawking, "is just another name for the prejudices that we have been brought up with." As for that which is tried and true, could it be, instead, tired and false?

The Fundamental "New Idea" Rule: When confronted with an off-the-wall idea from some nut job lunatic—even if that "lunatic" is you!—remember:

Don't reject that acorn-of-an-idea, then later wonder why you don't have any trees.

Problem: The average payout for medical malpractice claims has more than doubled in the past 10 years, the cost for malpractice insurance increasing by 15 to 40 percent each year.

Among physicians, solutions vary—from going without malpractice insurance ("going bare") to countersuing patients to having them sign waivers promising not to sue the physician or his corporation. More radical still, reports the *Wall Street Journal,* insurers are "rethinking the traditional approach known as 'defend and deny.' " Instead, they're "beginning to urge their clients to acknowledge errors and apologize"—a revolutionary concept known as "extreme honesty."

Why would a hospital or physician admit to having done something wrong? Because it makes fiscal sense.

In fact, reports the *Wall Street Journal,* "studies show that a majority of malpractice suits are brought not necessarily because of a bad outcome in treatment but because patients and their families felt medical staff either lied about it or tried to stonewall them afterward." Meanwhile, a policy of "extreme honesty" can help reduce costs. At the Veterans' Administration hospital in Lexington, Kentucky, its Sorry Works program has been in effect since the late 1980s, resulting in average settlements that are astonishingly low—just 16 percent of the national VA average. As a 1999 editorial in the journal *Annals of Internal Medicine* concluded, Lexington's Sorry Works program "seems to be the rare solution that is both ethically correct and cost-effective."

But maybe that just works for Veterans' hospitals, you say? At Johns Hopkins hospital, it's been estimated that a newly instituted "extreme honesty" policy helped reduce payments related to legal claims by 30 percent in a single year. And the University of Michigan Health System, which began its own version of Sorry Works in 2002, has seen legal actions pending against the system drop by more than 50 percent. As Rick Boothman, the system's chief risk officer puts it: “Patients are far more forgiving than we give them credit for.” Imagine. Having the nerve to even *entertain* such a radical, hard-to-believe-anyone-would-ever-even-*consider*-this approach. And yet . . . it works.

Creativity requires the freedom to consider ‘unthinkable’ alternatives, to doubt the worth of cherished practices. Every organization, every society is under the spell of assumptions so familiar that they are never questioned, least of all by those most intimately involved.

—John W. Gardner

If you see in any given situation only what everybody else can see, you can be said to be so much a representative of your culture that you are a victim of it.

—S. I. Hayakawa

Where all men think alike no one thinks very much.

—Walter Lippman

TRUE STORY

In 1996, a New York publisher thought it was a "Bad idea!" when the author of a forthcoming book, Harvey MacKay, proposed the title, *How to Swim With the Sharks Without Being Eaten Alive*. So MacKay spent his own money to take a poll among book buyers. Their favorite title? The same as MacKay's, minus the words "How to." *Swim With the Sharks Without Being Eaten Alive* went on to sell nearly 2 million copies. In other words: "Good idea!"

So how can you tell if it's a "Good Idea" or a "Bad Idea"?

Sometimes you can't—until you play it out.

Rachmaninoff thought his *Piano Concerto Number 2* was a disaster, considering parts of it "absolutely repulsive." And yet, it turned out to be one of his most popular works.

Joni Mitchell originally thought "Both Sides Now" was "a failure." (She later admitted, "I was not a good judge of my early material.") And actor John Malkovich confessed he almost didn't sign on for *In the Line of Fire* (1993) or *Places in the Heart* (1984), both of which, he says, "turned out really well." "The main point," says Malkovich, "is that you don't know. You just don't know."

"I can finish a movie I think is great work," says Woody Allen, "and it'll end up meaning nothing to people. They think it's insipid, pretentious, stupid, and they don't come to see it. On the other hand, I'll make films I'm humiliated by . . . But people will say, 'You're wrong, it's saying something to us.' "

TRUE STORY

Describing the first cut of Woody Allen's *Annie Hall*, film editor Ralph Rosenblum called it a "chaotic collection of bits and pieces that seemed to defy continuity." "Just for a moment," recalled cowriter Marshall Brickman, "I had a sense of panic: we took a chance, and it didn't work; we will be humiliated; is there any way to stop the project?" Eventually, about forty-five minutes of film were cut, new scenes were written, and *Annie Hall* went on to win four Academy Awards, including Best Screenplay.

"Thank God," says Allen, "the public only sees the finished product."

CHAPTER TAKE-A-WAYS

Never reject an idea simply because it sounds "crazy" or goes against conventional standards. Besides, all too often: *X becomes Y becomes "Why didn't we say YES to X in the first place?"*

- Learn to say YES! to a new idea, then see where it takes you.
- Be willing to change or adapt your idea. Ideas, like acorns, need time to grow and evolve.

11

Look for ELEGANT Solutions

What's an ELEGANT solution? Nothing less than the gold standard for winning solutions: a solution that is economical, unexpected, and inevitable. Consider the following:

Splitting the Baby: King Solomon, it could be argued, was the creator of the original, incredible elegant solution. What do you do when BOTH women say they're the mother? *Tell 'em you'll cut the baby in half—then WATCH what happens.*

Splitting the Cake: What do you do when two children each want be sure they're getting their fair share of a piece of cake? *Have one child cut it . . . the other one choose.* That's what you call an incredible ELEGANT solution.

Beating the Check: Picasso used to pay for smaller items—lunch, a carton of cigarettes—with a check. Why a check? Because no one would cash a check for a relatively small amount if it were signed by Picasso. (Allegedly, Clark Gable did much the same around Hollywood.)

In *A Mathematician's Apology* (1940), G. H. Hardy describes a "good proof" as having "a very high degree of unexpectedness, combined with inevitability and economy. The argument takes so odd and surprising a form . . . there is no escape from the conclusions."

**What's an elegant solution?
A solution that's economical,
unexpected, AND inevitable.**

Edwin Land believed that any problem could be solved by "using only the materials in the room." In fact, using only what's "in the room" provides your solution with the element of economy, an essential ingredient for an elegant solution.

In the movie *Apollo 13* (1995), Jim Lovell (Tom Hanks) and crew are slowly poisoning the cabin atmosphere with their own carbon dioxide. Back in Houston, the head engineer gathers a small team around a table and dumps out an assortment of odds and ends, explaining that these items duplicate those available to the astronauts. The engineers' mission? "We've gotta find a way to make this [large, square filter] fit into the hole for this [smaller, cylindrical filter] using nothing but [the items on the table]." Charged with figuring out how to "put a square peg in a round hole," their final product isn't pretty, but it works. By combining a plastic bag, cardboard from a flight manual, a hose from a pressure suit, duct tape, and a sock, they "solved" the astronauts' problem "using only the materials in the room"—in this case, the contents of the spacecraft.

TRUE STORY

One morning, having told this story at a conference the day before, I was approached by a woman who'd been in the audience. "Remember what you told us," she began, "about solving any problem using 'only the materials in the room?' This morning, I went to take a shower when I realized I'd forgotten my shower cap. And there wasn't a disposable one from the hotel, either. So I looked around the room and I saw the ice bucket, with a plastic bag draped over the edge. I put the bag over my head—and it worked!"

In *What Do* You *Care What Other People Think?*, physicist Richard Feynman recalls being part of a Presidential Commission charged with determining the cause of the space shuttle Challenger disaster in 1986, an explosion that killed seven astronauts. After just a few days of participating in the hearings, Feynman was onto something. He wondered if the O-rings, which showed "scorching" in preflight tests, were somehow responsible. He writes: "In ordinary circumstances, such as sealing oil in the motor of an automobile . . . [a]n O-ring just sits there, in a fixed position. But in the case of the shuttle, the gap *expands* as the pressure builds up in the rocket . . . [T]o maintain the seal, the rubber has to expand *fast* enough to close the gap—and during a launch, the gap opens in a fraction of a second. Thus the resilience of the rubber became a very essential part of the design."

What he next learned put the issue of resilience front and center: **The coldest outdoor temperature on previous takeoffs was 53 degrees; on the morning the Challenger took off the temperature was 28 or 29 degrees.** Feynman knew that the colder temperature would make the O-rings stiff and—he reasoned—make them slower to expand and contract. He asked NASA to provide him with information about "the effects over time of temperature on the resiliency of the O-rings." But the answer that came back was "of no use" at all. He continues: "I went back to my hotel. I'm feeling lousy and I'm eating dinner: I look at the table, and there's a glass of ice water. I say to myself, 'Damn it, I can find out about that rubber [without NASA's help]. I just have to try it!' " His idea was to use the very ice water supplied for drinking at their meetings. The only other thing he needed to find was a sample of the rubber, which, he learned, was part of a model the commission was to examine the next day. In other words: The two major components Feynman needed for his demonstration were *right in the room.* (The only things not in the room were a few incidentals: screwdrivers, pliers, and a small C-clamp, all of which were readily found at a local hardware store.)

At the next day's meeting, reports Feynman: "I squeeze the rubber in the C-clamp, and put them in the glass of ice water. After a few minutes . . . I take the clamp out, hold it up in the air, and loosen it." He continues: "I discovered that when you undo the clamp, the rubber doesn't spring back. In other words, for more than a few seconds, there is no resilience in this particular material when it is at a temperature of 32 degrees." Pleased with himself, he cheekily concludes: "I believe that has some significance for our problem."

In fact, Feynman's demonstration—his "selling" of his theory—was a *coup de grace* that all but solved the mystery of the disaster: an "elegant solution" devised, almost entirely, from only the materials "in the room."

What's part of every room that ever was or ever will be? The *room*—something you can also use.

Working on team building with sixty or so people, I split them into four groups—blindfolded. Their assignment? Holding hands, form a square. The winning group—for first forming a square (or something approximating a square)—didn't use something "in the room," they used the room itself. They found a corner of the room and used it as a guide to make their first 90 degree angle. After that, the rest was easy.

In 1959, Berry Gordy created a makeshift recording studio in his house in suburban Detroit and dubbed it "Hitsville." Short on cash, he used "the room" and everything in it: A hallway closet was turned into a vocal booth and a downstairs bathroom became the echo chamber. For sound effects, reports Gerald Posner in *Motown,* Gordy "tried everything from dragging chains along the wooden floors to having people jump and stomp, to striking screwdrivers against Coke bottles, to shaking jars of dried peas."

As Motown artist Stevie Wonder put it at the time:

Ya gots to work with what ya gots to work with.

Your success will also depend on how you define the word "room." It is simply the *physical* room and its contents? Or does it include the knowledge and abilities that are at your disposal? Consider the following:

- A pregnant woman sits at home with her three toddlers in a cramped apartment, fretting about her contractor husband having not been paid $3,000.00 for work he's performed. Distraught, and needing the money for food and rent, she does the only thing she can think of: She bundles up the kids and heads for the office of the man who employed her husband. She asks to see Mr. Big to get their money, but the receptionist explains that he'll be busy all day. "That's okay," she says. "We'll just wait." So the pregnant woman and her three toddlers camp out in the reception area. And every time someone comes in she makes it a point to let them know why she and her children are there. Sure enough. A few hours later her husband's check magically appears and she and her kids disappear.

Taking stock of her situation, our enterprising housewife saw the contents of her "room" as

1. Her children, and
2. Her pregnancy, which was obvious to anyone.

What was also in her "room" was

3. Her *chutzpah*—a kind of daring or audacity, allowing her to use her children (including the one in her belly) as emotional props, if you will, to generate much needed sympathy—and some cash.

- Legend has it that while shooting the movie *The Score* (2001), Marlon Brando arrived on the set one day without wearing pants. Why? So he could only be filmed from the waist up, ensuring a day of nothing but medium and closeup shots of the actor. *Long shots? Out of the question!*

  What was in Brando's room?

  1. His body
  2. His willingness to display that body, and
  3. His pants (having left them in his room).

- When British Petroleum (BP) sought to update its image and let people know it was focusing on renewable and alternative energy, it sought the advice of Landor, a branding consultancy. As Allen Adamson, managing director of Landor New York recalls, "BP wanted to dramatically transform the perception of the brand, to be known worldwide as the first environmentally friendly energy company—a bold, audacious goal." Landor's solution? *Instead of being known as "British Petroleum," use your* initials *to announce your new image:*

"BP: Beyond Petroleum." Think of it. You hear the phrase "Beyond Petroleum" and, suddenly, it's as if no other solution could possibly exist. That's when you know you've got an ELEGANT solution.

- A woman I know had been a litigator for fourteen years—and she hated it. Finally, she was determined to do something else with her life. I encouraged her to look at what was "in the room" (her training as a lawyer) but she just wouldn't hear of it. *Anything but law!* Her searching, in fact, went on for more than a year—from thinking about opening an art shop . . . to training as a psychologist . . . to working with something called flower essences, a collection of liquid "remedies" distilled from flowers. Finally, she found it—the answer she'd been looking for! She would become an estate planner, working to minimize her clients' estate taxes while helping them "to create a plan that is true to their values, goals and aspirations." She would also "work with them to plan a retirement that will meet their needs and desires; and counsel them in selecting guardians and making other decisions to ensure their children's well-being." Her primary qualifications for the job? Her training as a lawyer—something that had been "in the room" right from the start.

Limitations? Use them to your MAXIMUM ADVANTAGE. And remember:

Any problem can be solved using only the materials in the room. (Essential, however, is how you define the word "room.")

CHAPTER TAKE-A-WAYS

Edwin Land believed that any problem could be solved by using just what's "in the room." In fact, creating an elegant solution often depends on just that—using what's "in the room" to create a solution that is ECONOMICAL (absolutely, you're working with stuff that's already there), UNEXPECTED (*Who would have figured all this stuff we take for granted could create this great solution!*), and INEVITABLE (*Given the limitations we had, it's hard to imagine* anyone *could have solved it any better!*).

12

Try Some *EMPATHY*

"Opposites" thinking causes you to look at your situation as *differently* as possible. That change of perspective becomes even more fruitful when coupled with the magic of *empathy.*

Think of adults interacting with a baby or a small child. They crouch (making themselves appear smaller), speak in a higher-pitched voice than normal (closer to how a child sounds), and add a sing-song element to their speech (again, unconsciously moving towards being "child-like" in the way they talk and act). And all of this happens without a thought—a natural *empathy* for the child (the object of the adults' attention).

In *How to Drive Your Competition Crazy,* Guy Kawasaki writes about "a school that had trouble getting students to sign up for a course called "Home Economics for Boys." Taking the *school's perspective,* you might ask:

How do we get more students to sign up for "Home Economics for Boys?"

Taking the *students' perspective*—trying some *empathy*—you could more profitably ask:

Why don't more students want to sign up for "Home Economics for Boys?"

Looking at *that* question—seeing it with true empathic understanding—one answer becomes startlingly clear: *The title of the course is so darn boring it's pushing students away!* So the school changed the name of the course to "Bachelor Living" and, reports Kawasaki, "120 boys immediately signed up."

In *Sparks of Genius,* authors Robert and Michèle Root-Bernstein discuss how Einstein practiced empathy as he "pretended to be a photon moving at the speed of light, imagining what he saw and how he felt. Then he became a second photon and tried to imagine what he could experience of the first one." His goal, said Einstein, was to become "a little piece of nature." Not object and observer, but object and *experiencer.* Similarly, they report that Feynman "revolutionized quantum physics by asking himself questions such as 'If I were an electron, what would I do?'" And architect Louis Kahn was famous for asking, "What does this building want to be?"

The issue is empathy, taking a walk in someone else's shoes—even if that "someone else" does not wear shoes.

What kind of leash would you want if you were a dog? Certainly not a choke collar! Instead, the creators of the Gentle Leader Head Collar took a dog-centric, empathic approach. As the company's Web site explains: "Dogs are naturally 'pack' animals with a highly structured social order. One of the ways the 'pack leader' will demonstrate his position is to gently but firmly grasp a subordinate's muzzle in his mouth. This is a nonaggressive, very clear signal regarding who's the boss. The Gentle Leader's nose loop encircles your dog's muzzle in the same manner, letting him know in his own language that you are his leader. . . . Have you noticed how puppies seem to melt in relaxation when their mother picks them up at the back of the neck? Gentle Leader applies pressure to the back of the neck rather than the front of the throat, working with your dog's natural relaxation instinct with an amazing calming effect. Also, dogs tend to pull *against* pressure so the gentle pressure at the back of the neck causes the dog to pull backward, not forward." (In fact, I can attest that because of the Gentle Leader our own dog, Tux, gets a lot more walks—because they're easier on him—and on his owners.)

Let's apply Feynman's and Kahn's approaches to our examples:

If I were a dog, what would I do? Pull against my choke collar; it's only natural.
What would keep me from pulling? Being restrained by my pack leader.
What does this dog leash want to be? Leader of the pack.

If I were a student, what would I do? Run like heck from any course that sounds as boring as "Home Economics for Boys"!
What would keep me from running? Something that doesn't sound so girly.
What does this course want to be? Practical and appealing to boys.

Ask yourself these types of questions on your quest for solutions. They're not absolutes; they are, however, absolutely guaranteed to bring you closer to true empathic understanding and the solutions such understanding is sure to yield.

What happens when you have empathic understanding? After teaching at Harvard Medical School and the Boston Psychoanalytic Society and Institute, and serving as director of a children and adolescent program at the prestigious McLean Hospital for twenty years, child psychoanalyst Dr. Sebastiano Santostefano brought a new perspective to the art of analysis. Giving up working in a traditional "office" environment, he moved his practice to a rural setting where he and the children he works with can walk through the woods, lie on the grass, climb up a hill, play at a winding stream, and enjoy a pond stocked with fish and frogs. His peers call Santostefano's practice of working *outside* the office "cutting edge" and "groundbreaking," contributing to the therapist getting a broader "view of the range of the child's responses," among other benefits.

What happens when you lack empathic understanding? Consequences may include: your spouse or significant other complaining that you just don't "get it!"; getting divorced; having your customers leave you (or never showing up in the first place); and getting called names like "idiot" and "moron" (by your spouse or significant other and by others). Additionally, you may use names like "idiot" and "moron" to apply to everyone but you.

Have you ever noticed? Anybody going slower than you is an idiot, and anyone going faster than you is a moron.

—George Carlin

Tragedy is when I cut my finger. Comedy is when you fall into an open sewer and die.

—Mel Brooks

I'm trying to see things from your perspective but my head is too far up my a _ _!

—Tee shirt spotted while researching this chapter

TRUE STORY

I was driving a small sports car when I stopped for a red light, just behind a Humvee. A moment later, for no apparent reason, the Humvee started backing up and hit my car. The driver hopped out, looked at my broken headlight and screamed, "You're so low to the ground; how do you expect anyone to see you!?" To which I replied (fully aware of the joke I was launching): "You're so high up, how do you expect to see anyone down here!?" In other words: We each posed our questions in very different *nonempathic* ways, resulting, naturally, in very different answers—neither one even close to producing a fruitful answer.

ANOTHER TRUE STORY

It was a heat wave in August and traffic was at a standstill in downtown Los Angeles. My air conditioner wasn't working, I was hours away from home and there was no relief in sight. *This is horrible,* I thought, *not fair to me!* Just then I spotted a man with what looked like cerebral palsy, struggling to get his muscles to cooperate so he could make it across the street. Suddenly, I had a whole new perspective. *My life—stuck in traffic in the swelter of summer without AC—was, in comparison, very, very good.* What's needed is "empathic understanding"—a full appreciation of the other person's point of view.

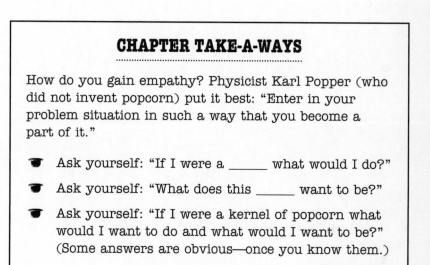

CHAPTER TAKE-A-WAYS

How do you gain empathy? Physicist Karl Popper (who did not invent popcorn) put it best: "Enter in your problem situation in such a way that you become a part of it."

- Ask yourself: "If I were a _____ what would I do?"
- Ask yourself: "What does this _____ want to be?"
- Ask yourself: "If I were a kernel of popcorn what would I want to do and what would I want to be?" (Some answers are obvious—once you know them.)

13

Look for the WORST Solution Possible

Instead of looking for the greatest idea or best solution, "opposites" thinking says:

Look for the WORST solution possible.

It's a fact: Most people have the ability to come up with a truly bad solution. (Sometimes, all you have to do is ask them for a *good* one.) But here's the good news: If you can come up with truly terrible ideas, you've got the ability to create great solutions. Consider the following:

A creative think tank was hired by the Woolmark Company to come up with an idea to promote the wearing of summer-weight wool clothing. Realizing this was no easy task, the creative team posed the following question:

What's the WORST way we can think of to promote summer-weight wool?

One suggestion (keep in mind they were looking for a BAD idea) was to let a bunch of sheep loose in Central Park. What's your vote?

___ **Good idea**

___ **Bad idea**

It's a terrible idea! That's where they started. They then asked themselves, How can we tweak this terrible idea into something pretty good?

Starting with their "worst" idea, the team "tweaked" it into this:

Let's have models wearing summer-weight wool clothing walk sheep on leashes down Madison Avenue!

Woolmark went for it and the publicity stunt snared more than eight million media impressions. (As one columnist opined: "Not baaad!")

I often use the "Worst Solution" exercise in my programs. We take a problem or issue that the client is facing and I encourage everyone in the group to try to come up with the "worst" solution they can think of. (This is not as easy as it sounds and it can take some time—along with my giving out F's for good ideas and A's for stinkers—for some people to catch on.) Finally, after listing all the really "bad" solutions we've come up with, we take a vote—voting for the absolute WORST of the worst. Once a "winner" is elected, we then take that WORST SOLUTION and tweak it into greatness. It may sound like a "magic act" but it works every time.

FOR EXAMPLE

One group I was working with—an association of independent manufacturers—had the problem of never having time to devote to strategic planning. Instead, they spent all their time putting fires out and keeping the business going. Our opening question? "How can we get the time to do strategic planning?" We then set about looking for the absolute WORST SOLUTION. The "winner?" The gentleman who said, "Go to Europe," sending the group into a roar of laughter.

"Okay," I said. "We have a winner! Now how can we 'tweak' that 'worst idea' into something pretty good?" Pretty soon we had a *very* satisfying answer: Instead of "chuck responsibility" or "leave the country and your troubles behind," we had a smart, reasonable course of action: *Take a three-day weekend out of town and devote your time to planning for the future.*

The room fell silent. No one, it seemed, had thought of the most obvious solution. Yet the solution arose the moment we stopped looking for a GREAT solution and sought out, instead, the WORST solution possible.

> Twice a year, since the 1980s, Bill Gates takes a break from his normal activities for "Think Week," a kind of Thoreau-in-the-woods retreat-from-the-every-day where he has time to "ponder the future of technology." He reads reports from Microsoft employees—as many as 100 in a week—e-mails his comments around the globe, and gets to plan for the future of his empire—without interruptions. Of course, it helps to be the richest man in the world to believe you really can afford to get away from it all. Then again, maybe you can't afford *not* to get away!

POP QUIZ

You're a matchbook manufacturer that's seen a steady decline in sales over the years. In the early 1970s—when the matchbook industry was at its peak—annual sales, nationwide, were at the $150 million mark. Why the decline in sales? No smoking bans in restaurants and bars and fewer people smoking overall.

QUESTION:

What's the WORST idea for increasing sales?

ANSWER:

Matchbooks without any matches inside.

FOLLOW-UP QUESTION:

Okay, now how can you tweak this "worst" idea into a pretty good idea? (Here's a hint: "If a matchbook didn't have any matches inside, would it just be empty or could you put something else in its place?")

"Well, let's see. We could put mints in there . . . gum . . . a single life saver . . . a poem . . . papers . . . a tiny notepad, perhaps."

And just like that you've got "Scratch Books" instead. Let's make a NOTE of that: "Create 'Scratch Books' and offer them as a line-extension. Who knows? They could outsell our matchbooks!"

There are times (as well) when a WORST idea is a pretty darn GOOD idea all by itself.

As a singer, for example, you could use your real name, Jerry Dorsey, or change it to the WORST name a singer could possibly have: Engelbert Humperdinck—an outstandingly bad idea that gave Dorsey a PR hook and helped turn him into a commercial success.

In 1999, I wrote a book called *The Worst Salesman in the World: Becoming the Best by Learning from the Worst.* Containing "field-tested can't-win techniques to make every sale disappear," its advice is clear: Study well what this book has to offer—and learn to do the opposite.

Similarly, reports film director Robert Altman: "People always ask who influenced me the most, and I think the true answer is . . . probably all the bad films I have seen by directors whose names I promised not to remember because I would say [to myself]: 'I'm never going to do *that.*' "

Author's Footnote: While I still consider *The Worst Salesman in the World* to be a great "worst idea," it failed to catch on in the marketplace and lives mostly in a warehouse. (At least for now.) Meanwhile, I derive some degree of comfort from the artist M. C. Escher, who famously said: "Only those who attempt the absurd will achieve the impossible. I think it's in my basement . . . let me go upstairs and check."

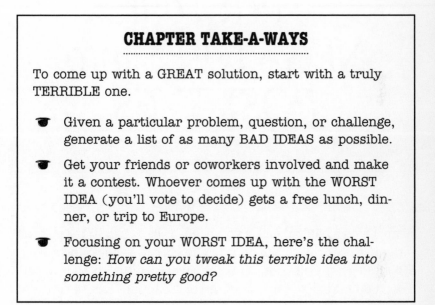

CHAPTER TAKE-A-WAYS

To come up with a GREAT solution, start with a truly TERRIBLE one.

- Given a particular problem, question, or challenge, generate a list of as many BAD IDEAS as possible.
- Get your friends or coworkers involved and make it a contest. Whoever comes up with the WORST IDEA (you'll vote to decide) gets a free lunch, dinner, or trip to Europe.
- Focusing on your WORST IDEA, here's the challenge: *How can you tweak this terrible idea into something pretty good?*

14

Turn Your NEGATIVES into POSITIVES

Armed with a bat and ball, a young boy calls out, "I'm the greatest hitter in the world!" Then he tosses up his ball, swings, and misses. *He tries again.* Calls out, "I'm the greatest hitter in the world!" Tosses up his ball, swings, and misses. Calls out, "I'm the greatest hitter in the world!" Tosses up his ball, swings, misses again. Calls out:

"I'm the greatest PITCHER in the world!"

In other words . . .

Think of your NEGATIVES as POSITIVES waiting to be DISCOVERED.

For most of its early history, Nevada had the smallest population of any state in the Union, except for Alaska. And there wasn't much to attract new people. So the legislature enacted a series of liberal divorce laws, combined with a minimal three-month residency requirement. Soon, the divorce business became the leading tourist attraction for towns like Reno and Las Vegas—as well-to-do folk came to get divorced and spend lots of money during their three month stay.

Nevada also made it easier to get married, offering "instant marriage, around the clock," an industry that thrived until the Depression hit. With tourism taking a hit, the Nevada legislature acted swiftly: It reduced its residency requirement to six weeks—and legalized gambling. Not only did Nevada's divorce business more than double, the state established itself as a desirable destination, even if you didn't need a divorce. There was gambling, entertainment, and an overall feeling of "anything goes" that lives on today.

Nevada's secret formula? Take a NEGATIVE—very few people and a challenging climate—and turn it into a POSITIVE cash flow. (More recently, states like Minnesota and West Virginia have taken the lead in turning a so-called negative—wind—and harnessing it into cash-generating windmills. In fact, studies have concluded that the combined wind power found in South Dakota, North Dakota, and Texas is—if properly harnessed—sufficient to generate enough electricity for the entire United States.)

TURNING A NEGATIVE INTO A FORTUNE

In 1951, while driving his family from Tennessee to vacation in Washington, Kemmons Wilson grew annoyed with the shabby lodgings he found en route. Making matters worse, he was forced to pay $2 extra for each of his five children. His negative experience fueling his resolve, Wilson became determined to start his own hotel chain—and not charge extra for children. The result? Holiday Inn—a chain of motels that gave millions of parents, and their children, a friendly, affordable place to stay, and became, as

Time magazine called it, "the most popular home away from home."

TURNING A NEGATIVE INTO A CAR

Twenty years ago, Glen McIntyre was a policeman in California. Then a drunk driver hit his motorcycle and he's been in a wheelchair ever since. Today, Glen is a speaker and trainer in the field of disability and diversity issues. He tells the following story about when he and his wife visited their local BMW dealership to shop for a car:

"As my wife walked onto the lot, and I rolled in my wheelchair, we headed toward a group of salespersons who were standing around waiting for customers. One by one they all looked away from us. Some even started walking away. (At least they weren't running!) *Can you imagine?* Here was a group of car salespersons waiting for customers—and here were my wife and I being totally ignored. An hour later—*an hour later*—we left the dealership without anyone having offered to help us. Not a soul tried to sell us a car."

Glen's first reaction was "frustration, even some anger." Then he began to wonder: *How many other salespersons have ignored a potential customer based solely on their first impression?* As Glen explains, "There are 54 million people in this country with disabilities; if you include their immediate family members you're looking at about 125 million potential buyers—what I like to call, 'the largest untouched market in the world!' So instead of complaining, I decided to offer a solution instead." He met with some local dealers and wound up selling them on producing a training video about dealing with people with disabilities. Not only did Glen turn a negative into a positive, he traded his services for a brand new BMW.

As Glen likes to say, "Always there is a way!"

TURNING A NEGATIVE INTO A BOOK (AND A MOVIE)

After having written a critically acclaimed first novel, *The Mysteries of Pittsburgh* (1988), Michael Chabon got a hefty advance and soon began work on his second novel. But four and a half years, four drafts, and more than 600 pages later, he realized "it wasn't working" and finally gave up on it. Tired, frustrated, and worried, he recalls: "I started to think, 'Oh, my God, I'm going to become one of those writers who are working on the same book for ten years.' Then I started thinking, 'Well, what would that be like? Who does it happen to and why does it happen?' " That set Chabon's creative wheels in motion. Seven months later, he had his first draft of *Wonder Boys,* a book that would do well in the marketplace and become a successful movie starring Michael Douglas.

By turning his problems into pages, Chabon was taking a well-trodden literary path—taking personal "disaster" and using it as grist for the mill: Alcohol, bulimia, cancer, drug addiction (and that's just *a* through *d*). Whatever the writer's struggle or malady, with pluck, and a bit of luck, can often be turned into "profitable" experience. Same goes for business failures, bad investments (of time, energy, or money), and other human foibles. As the old saying goes, *Live and learn*. Or, if you're enterprising, *Live, learn, and EARN from your experience.*

TRUE CONFESSION

When I first started out as a speaker, I found myself spending *way too much energy* trying to remember *What comes next?* So I decided to "use my fault." The solution? In my *Shake That Brain!* presentations I would hand out a series of prompt cards to someone in the audience, asking that he or she shuffle them as best they could. Once shuffled, I'd ask that they call out the title of the first card on their deck—say, "Is it a good idea to question your assumptions?" or "Good idea or bad idea?" No matter what the card read, that's what I would talk about. Soon as I finished a topic, I'd ask them to read what the next card said. "That way," I'd tell my audience, "it's my job to be as creative as I can, making sure the whole presentation makes sense—regardless of the order of the cards. And because we have a dozen cards here, the number of possible combinations is more than a million. So the likelihood that I've encountered these cards, in this particular order, is very, very low." The result? I'd taken my "fault" (my struggle to remember *What comes next?*) and turned it into a neat little challenge—seeing just how clever Saltzman could be on his feet, while letting the audience know, "Odds are, this is a show I've never presented before, and I'm about to see it—just like you—for the first time ever."

In 1984, Ronald Reagan was seventy-three years old when he ran for reelection against Walter Mondale. Asked in their second presidential debate if he thought age should be a factor in the election, Reagan replied: "I will not exploit for political purposes my opponent's youth and inexperience." Turning a negative into a POSITIVE, Reagan landed a knockout punch and won the election by landslide.

TASTING DISABILITY ENABLES FORTUNE

BEN: I've never had a very good sense of smell, and if you don't have that, you don't have a good sense of taste. When we began, the game was for Jerry to make a flavor I could taste with my eyes closed. To do that, he had to make ice creams that were intensely flavored. Also, because of this disability, I have an excellent sense of mouth feel. Creaminess and crunchiness are very important to people who can't taste.

JERRY: This led to our putting bigger than standard chunks of fruit and candy into our ice creams. It turned out that people really liked these highly flavored, extra-chunky ice creams. We were offering them something unique.

I couldn't play like everyone else. Guitarists have skinny fingers. Look at these: I got meat hooks. Size 12 glove. I play drum licks on the guitar.

—Bo Diddley

I was a good pianist, but I wouldn't go to Carnegie Hall and try to fool anybody. . . . So I used my ability to influence people to laugh and combined music and words.

—Victor Borge

Use your faults.

—Edith Piaf

LESS MONEY = MORE CREATIVITY

Peter Hedges, who directed *Pieces of April* (2003), originally had a go-ahead to make the film for $6 million at United Artists. But a month before shooting was to begin, the studio pulled the plug. Enter InDigEnt Films, willing to make Hedges's film—in digital video instead of film, in seventeen days instead of forty, and for a minuscule price tag of $300,000.

In other words:

His budget was slashed 95%

The result? *Pieces of April* won prizes from the National Board of Review, the Sundance Film Festival and earned $2.3 million in its first two months. As Gary Winick, a cofounder of InDigEnt, explains it: "When you're forced to do something with less money, you're forced to use your imagination and things usually turn out even better."

In the movie *Rocky* (1976), Sylvester Stallone takes Adrianne (Talia Shire) ice skating at an indoor rink. Because the rink is closed, Rocky gets special "permission" from a friend of his who works there. In fact, the scene—as written—called for a full complement of extras to be skating at the same time. But extras cost money that just wasn't in the shoestring budget. So now you know why that rink was closed when Rocky showed up. *It cost less money that way!* And the scene was just as effective—probably more. Because it suddenly became more *intimate* than it ever would have been.

WAITING STINKS?

WAITING IS <u>GOOD</u> FOR YOU!

A public affairs official for Long Beach Airport in California (twenty plus miles from Los Angeles International) touts the benefits of using this secondary airport, explaining: "If it's sunny, people can sit outside while they wait and watch the planes take off and land." What she doesn't mention is that the airport has virtually NO inside waiting space. So you're pretty much FORCED to wait outside—either on aluminum benches or at half a dozen patio tables scattered by the tarmac. (A picnic it's not.) However, given the same set of negatives:

"what if . . ."

What if the airport turned its negative into a POSITIVE that really made it different and unique? Like an outdoor space that truly invited you to be outdoors. (Years ago, I stayed at a hotel in New York City that had such a small room all I could say was: "It's the kind of room that really makes you want to go out and see the City!")

I see . . . a waterfall . . . footbaths and towels . . . foot massages . . . attendants dressed in Roman togas feeding grapes to waiting passengers reclined on the beach . . . (Too far out, you say? As poet Wallace Stevens would respond, "One must go too far to see what would suffice." Besides, maybe a waterfall, footbaths and Roman togas aren't "too far out" at all!) *The airport as a day at the beach? Why not!? A beautiful beach right there at Long* ***Beach*** *Airport! Wait, I see the billboard: "Come visit us at Long Beach Airport. Where it really is . . . like a day at the beach!"* (See: "Beach Deprived," page 73.)

WHAT HAPPENS WHEN YOU CAN'T AVOID THE NEGATIVE? GIVE IT A POSITIVE SPIN!

Sometimes, you just can't avoid that negative and have to face it head on. Advertisers excel at this—taking a negative and giving it a positive spin. Consider, for example, the provocative question:

"Are you lucky enough to need glasses?"

—Lens Crafters

Or imagine a magazine ad that features a group of mountain bike riders, muddied, but happy. Underneath, the caption reads:

"Lots of the more popular leisure activities of today's younger workers involve getting muddy to a certain extent. And to that end, we proudly boast over 121,364 square miles of pure, unspoiled dirt."

—New Mexico Development Department

In 2002, Ikea launched a $40 to $50 million "Unböring" furniture campaign, aimed at convincing consumers that furniture can be "disposable." As one ad read:

If you're in a bad relationship with old furniture but don't put an end to it,

you are crazy.

By hitching a ride on the "disposable" clothing bandwagon (think Old Navy), Ikea is turning a NEGATIVE (products that don't last very long) into a POSITIVE (your ability to replace them whenever you'd like). "You buy the T-shirt at Old Navy that's good for eight weeks and, great, you throw it out. These aren't cherished pieces." So noted Candace Corlett, a principal of the consulting company, WSL Strategic Retail.

Sound crazy? Unable to decide what we *really* wanted for the den, my wife and I were recently given a similar "disposable" pitch at a local "chic but cheap" furniture den in Los Angeles. It's not like it's going to last you the rest of your life. But who cares? You'll grow tired of it in a couple of years and replace it!

And yes, we bought it.

AC-CEN-TU-ATE THE NEGATIVE

Manufacturer W. K. Buckley is proud to say that for eighty years Canadians have hated its cough syrup. In fact, advertisements for its product have traditionally employed the negative. From:

Relief is just a yuck away.

To:

Not new. Not improved.

Now making inroads into the United States, the company declares in American print ads:

**Buckley's Mixture. It tastes awful.
And it works.**

That kind of "negative" advertising has helped make Buckley's Canada's No. 3 cough-syrup maker.

Is Buckley's the first to adopt an "opposites" approach to promoting its product? Hardly. "Negative" ad campaigns have included:

- Listerine mouthwash—"the taste you love to hate."
- The Volkswagen Beetle—"ugly as ever."
- "With a name like Smucker's it's got to be good."
- Avis—"We're Number 2."

What do you say about a company that is using its advertising dollars to trumpet its negatives? I'd say that's a company:

- Questioning assumptions (*Do we HAVE TO stress positives?*)
- Applying an "opposites" approach (*Bad taste, Bad looks, Bad name*) and, as a result:
- Grabbing our attention. (*You're NOT Number One? That's different!*)

Gone to prison? *Good for you!*

When country singer/songwriter Merle Haggard was just starting out, he told Johnny Cash that he lived in fear that his San Quentin prison record would be exposed and ruin his career. (In fact, when Cash played San Quentin in the late '50s, Haggard was in the audience.) Cash's advice to the worried ex-con? Instead of *hiding* from it, try *writing* about it. That led Haggard to write and record "Mama Tried," which became a No. 1 hit on the country charts in 1968 and remains one of Haggard's most popular songs. That is, "Mama Tried" to reform him when he was a teenager but he just wouldn't listen—though he did wise up (and cash in) when Cash set him straight.

In other words . . .

GO WITH THE FLOW.

"Go with the flow" is not just the creation of California laid-back thinking. It relates as well to the ancient Japanese system of self-defense, Aikido, where circular movements are used to redirect an opponent's force, using his strength and weight to work against him. Think of the "go with the flow" approach as another way of taking a negative and *redirecting* it.

TRUE STORY

A woman owned a toy store by a local park. As luck would have it, dog walkers started making it a habit of congregating right in front of her store, blocking her entrance, obscuring her display window from passers-by and, she figured, costing her money. Her first question, naturally enough, was:

How do I get these loiterers away from my store?

Faced with the prospect of asking them to move, she just couldn't bring herself to the task. Finally, she solved her problem by putting a sign in the window that read:

**Free Dog Biscuits.
Come on in!**

Dog walkers came in for a treat for their dogs, spotted impulse items or greater, and generated new sales. By taking her negative—"loiterers"—and *redirecting* them, that wise store owner turned her PROBLEMS into PROSPECTS.

The Traveling Wilburys v. The Traveling Wilburys

Rock 'n rollers Roy Orbison, Bob Dylan, George Harrison, Jeff Lynne, and Tom Petty decided to form their own band and call themselves The Traveling Wilburys. Before they went on tour, though, they heard from a group of weekend rockers that had been using the same name, The Traveling Wilburys, long before Orbison and friends teamed up. To avoid legal battles, the star-studded group proposed a "go with the flow" solution: the more-famous Wilburys invited the garage-band Wilburys to go on tour with them, as the opening act for a select number of big-venue gigs. What did the garage band have to offer? Legitimate rights to use the *Traveling Wilburys* name and a fun PR angle that could help sell tickets—for everyone.

Leo and the Pirates

After creating Bakelite plastics, Leo Baekeland (1863–1944) was burdened with continuing legal battles in an effort to stop people from infringing on his patents. He won every case against these "pirates," as he called them. But he didn't stop there—he then used the aikido concept to join forces with adversaries. If he thought they were doing something that could benefit Bakelite, he offered to bring them into the Bakelite empire. (For Baekeland, it wasn't so much *If you can't beat 'em, join 'em,* as *If you can beat 'em, beat 'em. Then join 'em!*)

Ella and Mack

In 1960, Ella Fitzgerald was singing "Mack the Knife" to a crowd in Berlin. It was the first time she had sung the song and she forgot some of the lyrics. Her choice was clear: Do I stop and apologize—admit that I have no idea where I'm headed—or do I "go with the flow" and try to make the best of things?

Ella kept going, making up new words as she went along. They rhymed, fit the music, and her performance was a tour de force. Fortunately, the show was being recorded and a record was released later that year. As a reward for her daring to improvise lyrics to replace those she'd forgotten—turning a negative into a positive—Ella's recording of "Mack the Knife" won her a Grammy Award for Best Female Vocal Performance.

Got a Negative?
Be POSITIVE.

Even better . . .

Be Negative.

—Kenneth Cole campaign against HIV

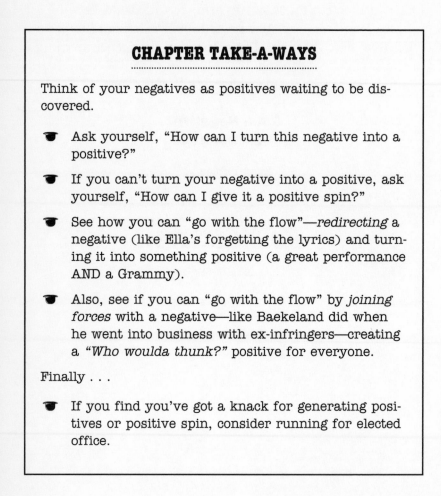

CHAPTER TAKE-A-WAYS

Think of your negatives as positives waiting to be discovered.

- Ask yourself, "How can I turn this negative into a positive?"
- If you can't turn your negative into a positive, ask yourself, "How can I give it a positive spin?"
- See how you can "go with the flow"—*redirecting* a negative (like Ella's forgetting the lyrics) and turning it into something positive (a great performance AND a Grammy).
- Also, see if you can "go with the flow" by *joining forces* with a negative—like Baekeland did when he went into business with ex-infringers—creating a *"Who woulda thunk?"* positive for everyone.

Finally . . .

- If you find you've got a knack for generating positives or positive spin, consider running for elected office.

15

Ask Yourself, "What Can I IMITATE?"

Originality is nothing but judicious imitation.
—Voltaire

Looking for a great solution? Ask yourself, "What can I 'borrow' or imitate that *already* exists?"

The story is well known: As an undergraduate at Yale, Frederick W. Smith got a C for a paper he wrote proposing the idea of overnight deliveries. Nonplussed, Smith went on to found FedEx. What most people *don't* know, however, is that the idea was definitely "borrowed." As Smith has explained, his "innovation" came from "taking an idea from the telecommunications and banking industries, and applying that idea to the transportation business. Using a central clearing house, along with a hub-and-spoke system of dissemination, enabled us to deliver, point-to-point, anywhere in the United States—absolutely, positively overnight."

Henry Ford did not invent the assembly line. (Oliver Evans had already automated a flour mill.) Ford and his men got their inspiration elsewhere—from Chicago's stockyards, where they studied the Swift "disassembly" line. All Ford had to do was borrow Swift's idea and do the "opposite"—turn a disassembly line into an *assembly* line—thereby dramatically reducing the time and money it took to produce a Model T. Time to assemble a car's chassis and engine, for example, dropped from 12.5 man-hours to less than six. ("I invented nothing new," admitted Ford. "I simply assembled into a car the discoveries of other men behind whom were centuries of work.")

Now imagine you know someone whose job is working at an automobile assembly line. One day he tells you about a "dream" he has—taking the concept of the assembly line and applying it to making music. *Sound absurd?* Listen to this:

> *My dream for a hit factory was quickly taking form, a concept that had been shaped by principles I had learned working at the Lincoln-Mercury assembly line. At the plant the cars started out as just a frame, pulled along on conveyor belts until they emerged at the end of the line—brand spanking new cars rolling off the line. I wanted the same concept for my company, only with artists and songs and records. I wanted a place where a kid off the street could walk in one door an unknown and come out another a recording artist—a star.*

The writer is Berry Gordy, founder of Motown Records, as recalled in his biography, *To Be Loved.* Corporate headquarters ("Hitsville") started out in a small two-story house in suburban Detroit that Gordy and his family also lived in; yet Motown Records soon became a hit maker for artists like the Supremes, Stevie Wonder, Marvin Gaye, the Marvelettes, Smokey Robinson, the Temptations, and others. And Gordy—most definitely—used the assembly line as a model for his hit-making factory: Songs were written according to a standardized format (lyrics in the present tense) and there was an in-house band ("The Funk Brothers") giving each tune the same distinctive Motown rhythm and sound. Much like a car manufacturer—dependant on lots of people buying the same car—Gordy's sole focus was on churning out top forty hits in assembly-line fashion.

Schooled on the Lincoln-Mercury assembly line, Gordy's perspective was commercial all the way. To help convince buyers to want to get the latest Motown record, Gordy made it as simple as possible—by creating that "Motown sound" that stayed the same, record to record, and by combining and rearranging elements of existing hits to create "new" hits that instantly gave listeners a comfortable déjà vu experience. If automobile makers only had to *modify* their cars year to year, why, reasoned Gordy, couldn't he do the same with his records?

As for the performers, their moves were strictly choreographed—from dramatic stage entrances to the synchronized Motown moves—to suit each song. Finally, each Motown act was "polished" by a team that dressed them, taught them about makeup, how to sit and carry themselves, even how to get out of a car. That final "polish," writes Posner, was inspired by "the movie-studio charm schools of the thirties and forties." The entire process—forging artists and songs that each bore an uncanny resemblance to each other—was, in fact, much like the assembly line model Gordy had imagined, turning unknowns to stars and making Motown a fortune.

Musicians, in fact, have a long history of "borrowing" from others—like Stravinsky, studying Mozart's operas and calling himself "Mozart's continuer"; Elvis Presley—borrowing black rhythm and blues; Ray Charles—borrowing gospel music while adding rhythm and blues; rap music—borrowing rhythm and blues, then adding poetry; Paul Simon—borrowing South African pop music and combining it with rock 'n roll for his album, *Graceland*; Beck—borrowing rap rhythms, hip-hop, blues, country, hard rock, and anything else that makes a sound and putting it into a kind of aural blender; music samplers—

borrowing actual pieces from other people's recordings and mixing them into their own.

And so on, and so on, and so on, and so on.

In commerce, it's much the same—"borrowing" from others:

The Ziploc food-storage bag—"borrowing" the zipper concept from, well, zippers.

The Teflon-coated iron—"borrowing" from the Teflon-coated stick-free frying pan.

Furniture fabrics—"borrowing" menswear-inspired pinstripes and houndstooth.

A pet-grooming shop—"borrowing" the idea of a restaurant with an open kitchen, or a viewing window, and creating a grooming shop where passersby can watch through the window as a dog or cat gets attended to. (A smart way to advertise and to demonstrate what great treatment the animals receive.)

The Kinesis keyboard and foot-pedal—"borrowing" the idea of a foot pedal from sewing machines. Now, instead of hitting the Shift key, I can tap on my foot-pedal TO MAKE EVERYTHING UPPER CASE without adding a single key stroke. Since capital letters, and their attendant "extra" key strokes contribute significantly to carpal tunnel syndrome, reducing these key strokes is a major achievement. (Or go full tilt with a NoHands mouse, moving complete mouse control to your feet. It may sound "absurd," but people swear by it; at least those on the NoHands Web site, www.footmouse.com.)

Starbuck's—"borrowing" the cafe scene from espresso bars in Italy.

Mega bookstores and public libraries—"borrowing" from Starbuck's by offering Booko Frappucinos, Library Lattes, and other coffee offerings (sometimes, by including an actual Starbuck's right inside).

And, once again, **Starbuck's**—borrowing a certain "hip-ness" factor (and making money) by selling the music of Ray Charles and others.

POP QUIZ

What can a famous museum learn or "borrow" from McDonald's?

Answer:

Franchising. The Guggenheim Museum, long based in New York, now has branches in Las Vegas and Bilbao, Spain (where the owners pay a licensing fee). Meanwhile, discussions are currently underway about Guggenheim "satellites" being built in Guadalajara and Singapore. When a reporter asked Thomas Krens, director of the Guggenheim, where his priorities were—"home or abroad"—Krens, wisely avoiding either/or thinking, replied: "Both."

The trick, if you will, is to constantly be surveying your landscape (everywhere you go, everything you read, see, listen to, or overhear), asking yourself: "What's here that I can 'borrow' and apply to my situation?" In fact, the more on the "look out" you are, the better your chances for stumbling onto something good. In grade school, when we learned a new word, we often discovered—as if by magic—that suddenly our new vocabulary word was everywhere we went. People were using it in conversation, you'd hear it on the radio, see it in books you were reading. Yet it was there . . . all along. Likewise, so are lots and lots of solutions. All you need is to pay attention.

Observing

In the late 1950s, a woman named Ruth Handler gained a novel—and profitable—idea by observing her daughter at play, noticing that her daughter preferred playing with teenage dolls and their fashion accessories, even though the dolls and accessories were only paper cutouts. Handler's idea was to create a grown-up doll, a model for authentic clothing and accessories, a surrogate for a little girl's fantasies of her future. The reception to Barbie—named after the Handlers' daughter—at the 1959 New York Toy Show was cool. Yet within eight years, the Barbie line would rack up $500 million in orders.

At about the same time that Handler made her money-winning observation, Bette Nesmith Graham was a secretary at a bank when, like Handler, she managed to "observe people in their daily lives" and "identify a need." She recalled: "I remember trying to make a little extra money by helping design the holiday windows at the bank. With lettering, an artist never corrects by erasing but always paints over the error. So I decided to use what artists use. I put some tempera waterbase paint in a bottle and took my watercolor brush to the office. And I used that to correct my typing mistakes." Her invention? Mistake Out, later renamed Liquid Paper.

Sam Farber, another keen observer, was a retired kitchenware manufacturer when he saw his wife, who had mild arthritis, struggle with gripping a potato peeler. This led Farber to wonder: "Why couldn't there be comfortable tools that are easy to use, not just for arthritis victims but for everybody?" After consulting with chefs, consumers, retailers, and (as reported on the OXO Web site) "a noted gerontologist . . . to help understand the needs of the users with special needs," Farber introduced the thick-handled, easier to grip, OXO potato peeler and nineteen other kitchen tools at the Gourmet Show in San Francisco. Like Barbie's debut some thirty years earlier, the reception was tepid. Farber recalled: "It was slow launching because they looked different and our price was higher. The [Good Grips] potato peeler was $6, and no one had paid that before."

While merchants were skeptical, consumers quickly embraced them: They looked cool and were a lot easier to use than their standard forbearers. Today, OXO utensils ("Tools you hold on to.") features more than 750 products that can be found in thousands of retail outlets nationwide. (The Good Grips potato peeler is still their leading product.)

Listening

According to *People* magazine, John Kilcullen, creator of the ***. . . For Dummies*** series of books, got the idea from a friend of his "who had overheard a customer asking a software-store clerk for a book about DOS (the famously confusing but now arcane computer operating system)—'something really low-level, for me—DOS for dummies.' But it wasn't until 1990, when he was hired by publishing giant IDG to cofound its book division, that he got to bet his career on it. 'I thought it was illustrative, funky, unconventional. And it really reflected the risk I wanted to take.' "

Carl Perkins was at a dance in the 1950s when he overheard a boy tell his dance partner, "Don't step on my suedes." No one knows the boy's name but everyone knows Perkins' signature song, "Blue Suede Shoes."

And **Paul McCartney** (who grew up listening to Carl Perkins's records) recalls: "I remember asking the chauffer once if he was having a good week. He said, 'I'm very busy at the moment. I've been working eight days a week.' And I thought, 'Eight days a week!' Now there's a title!"

Borrowing from Things That Exist

In 1947, Chuck Yeager broke the sound barrier in the Bell X-1 aircraft. At the time, various news stories referred to the plane as "a bullet with wings." No wonder. Engineers at Bell had observed that a fifty-caliber bullet remained fairly stable even as it flew at supersonic speed. So when they designed the X-1, they gave it a shape that pretty much mimicked the shape of that bullet.

Ron Johnson, Apple's senior vice-president for retailing, was searching for a new concept for Apple stores when he started thinking about Four Seasons and Ritz-Carlton hotels, places known for their exceptional service. That led Johnson and his team to create trademarked "Genius Bar" service counters for their retail stores. Above each service counter hangs the "atomic" symbol (popular in the '50s) of three intersecting ovals with the words: Genius Bar. Also, each "Genius Bar" bar features an electronic display of words of wisdom from intellectual biggies like Leonardo da Vinci and Michelangelo ("If people knew how hard I had to work to gain my mastery, it wouldn't seem wonderful at all.") Finally, each bar is staffed by Apple "Geniuses"—Johnson's idea for what to call their tech support staff—who work mostly on ailing laptops and ipods. (To make sure customers won't have to wait at the bar, so to speak, same-day free appointments can be scheduled online.) Apple's goal? To make sure their customers receive friendly, courteous, top-notch service worthy of the Ritz. (And when you find yourself chatting with a bona-fide "genius," you can't help but have some fun as well.)

Borrowing from Nature

Just as you can "borrow" from *things* that exist (a bullet, a disassembly line) or *ideas* that exist (franchising, hub-and-spoke distribution), you can also borrow from *nature* for solutions that have existed for millions of years. Known as biomimicry, the approach is just what it sounds like—looking to see what science or manufacturing can "mimic" from nature. For example:

> **Velcro**—mimicking those prickly cocklebursthat stick to you when you go hiking. Long considered a "negative," it took an enterprising person, Swiss engineer George de

Mestral, to observe how nature's tiny hooks could be applied to creating a breakthrough solution.

Camouflage clothing—Based on chameleons and other animals that camouflage themselves in nature—something people had noticed since the dawn of creation—it took an enterprising soul (painter and natural history buff Abbot Thayer) to understand the general principles and apply it to military camouflage, that is, animals (military personnel) seeking to disguise themselves from "predators" in the wilds.

Where has man (the manufacturer) borrowed from nature (the prototype)? For starters, consider the following pairs of nearly-identical "twins"—one from man, the other from nature.

From Man	From Nature
Camera lens and iris	Eyes
Windshield wiper	Eye lid
Wiper fluid	Tears
Coring or aerating lawns	Worms and insects that do the same
Ball joint	Shoulder joint
Microphone	Ear drum
Hypodermic needles	Snake fangs
Snowshoes	Penguins' feet
Frames of buildings	Animal skeletons
Hang gliders	Butterflies

As Einstein himself put it: "One thing I have learned in a long life: that all our science, measured against reality, is primitive and childlike."

One "problem-solving" technique is to ask yourself, *What in the natural world (plants, animals, forests, oceans, etc.) has already solved my problem incredibly well?* German botanist Dr. Wilhelm Barthlott at the University of Bonn did just that, asking himself, *How do white flowers keep so white and how can I apply it to the manufacture of a stays-bright-and-white type paint?* He learned, that ". . . the cleanest leaf of all—the white lotus—turned out to have tiny points on it, like a bed of nails. . . . When a speck of dust or dirt falls on the leaf, it teeters precariously on those points. When a drop of water rolls across the tiny points, it picks up the poorly attached dirt and carries it away." Nicknamed the "lotus effect," it's been formulated into a house paint called Lotusan. Currently available in Europe and Asia, Lotusan "is guaranteed to stay clean for five years without detergents or sandblasting." Next in line for the lotus effect? Roof shingles and car paint.

David Oakey, who designs commercial carpeting and textiles, told the *New York Times*: "The question we ask is, *How would nature solve this problem?* When you ask that question, you move in directions you never would have thought about." Consider, for example, a "biomimicked" carpet he designed called Entropy that "mimics" the intermixed shades and colors of a forest floor. Should a section of Entropy wear out or be stained, it can simply be "replaced" with no matching problems. As for other solutions that nature may offer, Oakey asks: "Can you do it without dye, but with refraction, like the feather of a bird?" "Can you make it like a snake skin, where instead of taking out the whole carpet you take a sliver off the top and replace that?"

POP QUIZ

Which would you prefer?

(a) Looking to yourself to "invent" solutions?
(b) Looking to 3.8 billion years of experience among constantly evolving molecular and biological systems to "discover" solutions that already exist?

In addition to "borrowing" from nature to inspire new products, we can *harness* nature to do our work for us, from photoelectric cells and windmills to underwater turbines powered by the ocean's endless waves. We can also look to the ecosystem itself, with its complex system of checks and balances designed to maintain a healthy environment and a renewable planet. (At least that was the plan.) In Fuzhou, China, for example, a sewage canal has been drastically cleaned up by a "living machine" consisting of plants, carp fish, and two strains of bacteria that work in harmony to restore the water to health. Genetically modified "nature" (though beyond the scope of this book) also holds promise. In Danbury, Connecticut, as reported by *Esquire* magazine in 2004, 160 genetically modified cottonwood trees work to clean up the poisonous ionic mercury waste left in the ground by "thirty-five former hat factories, notorious as the source of the 'Danbury shakes,' a kind of mad-hatter's disease." The trees actually thrive on the waste, "gobbling up deadly ionic mercury, metabolizing it, and then dispersing a less harmful form of elemental mercury into the atmosphere." Pioneered by Richard Meagher, director of the Molecular Genetics Instrumentation Facility at the University of Georgia, Meagher confided he's been called a "crackpot and a charlatan." *What else is new?*

How do you "make the connection"? How do you see or hear X and suddenly jump to your *eureka* y?

First, your mind needs to be sufficiently "open" or receptive to X. Think of it like soil that's been tilled and ready for planting. How do you "till" your mind? First, by reading this book—and by returning to it whenever you need to *Shake That Brain!* for a good creative jolt. You can also "till" your mind simply by maintaining—somewhere in your brain—the thought: *I need to be solving or working on such and such.* Having so "tilled" or "tuned" your brain to a particular frequency—say, Project X—you will now be infinitely more receptive to ideas or "signals" that may just cross your path.

German lighting designer Ingo Maurer (whose work has been exhibited in the Museum of Modern Art) told the *New York Times* that for inspiration he relies on "what he calls *hasard,* the French word for chance—unexpected moments when light makes a visual impression. . . . Such 'sense impressions,' as he calls them, can percolate for years before Mr. Maurer . . . finally translates them into a design. 'I wait until the moment comes . . . I don't try to force it.'"

Case in Point: The paragraph you just read was from an article I've been saving for nearly five years. I always thought, *Maybe I can use this somehow,* but I let the idea "percolate for years" until—just this morning—I discovered that it "finally translates" into my "design" for this book. *And now . . . back to Mr. Maurer.*

The *Times* continues: "His inspiration for Ya Ya Ho (1984), perhaps his most influential and copied design, was born on a New Year's Eve in Haiti." Maurer explains: "We came out into this little piazza, and there were two strings running across it, with one huge glass light bulb trying to fight the morning sun. I was so thrilled, because the bulb had no socket, and was soldered straight onto the wire. I could have stood there forever."

How do you find that next great idea? Take a walk in the woods, a trip to the beach, or spend some time at the Ritz-Carlton bar. Let your mind unwind and let *hasard,* or chance, show you the way.

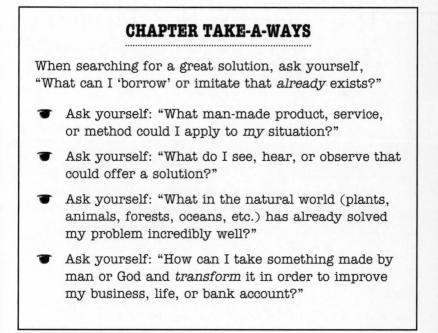

CHAPTER TAKE-A-WAYS

When searching for a great solution, ask yourself, "What can I 'borrow' or imitate that *already* exists?"

- Ask yourself: "What man-made product, service, or method could I apply to *my* situation?"
- Ask yourself: "What do I see, hear, or observe that could offer a solution?"
- Ask yourself: "What in the natural world (plants, animals, forests, oceans, etc.) has already solved my problem incredibly well?"
- Ask yourself: "How can I take something made by man or God and *transform* it in order to improve my business, life, or bank account?"

16

Ask Yourself, "What Would ______ Do?"

The ideas I stand for are not mine. I borrowed them from Socrates. I swiped them from Chesterfield. I stole them from Jesus. And I put them in a book. If you don't like their rules, whose would you use?

—Dale Carnegie

The process is simple: Choosing a mentor or someone in your field whose work you admire and respect, ask yourself: *What would ________ do?*

- Referring to his mentor, Johnny Carson, David Letterman says: "All of us who came after are pretenders . . . A night doesn't go by that I don't ask myself, 'What would Johnny have done?' "
- Twyla Tharp, in *The Creative Habit*, writes that early in her career "If one day I was stuck, I could ask myself, How would Martha [Graham] move? or What would [dance pioneer and choreographer] Doris Humphrey feel like? I could harness

their memory as easily as if it were my own, and use the things they were using to fashion my own solutions."

- Remember Feynman's excitement at realizing he could use ice water to test his theory for the Commission? ("'Damn it, *I* can find out about that rubber without NASA's help. 'I just have to try it!' ") *Great idea?* Great idea! But a moment later, he thinks: "'No, that would be gauche.' But then I think of Luis Alvarez, the physicist. He's a guy I admire for his gutsiness and sense of humor, and I think, 'If Alvarez was on the commission, he would do it, and that's good enough for me.' "

So there you go: If it's something your mentor would do, chances are it's "good enough" for you.

A note of caution: Getting inspiration or guidance is one thing; "aping" or "copying" quite another. As Tharp confesses: "When I was beginning, I would sometimes find myself solving problems in exactly the same way that teachers such as Martha Graham and Merce Cunningham solved them. I would catch myself and say, 'Wait a minute. That's how Martha or Merce would do it. We can't have that.' "

"Scratching among the paradigms" is fine, she says, unless "it turns you into an imitator rather than a creator."

Mark Urman, who worked as a publicity and marketing consultant for Harvey Weinstein, founder of Miramax Films, now leads the United States theatrical division of ThinkFilm, a Canadian independent. "We don't always do what Harvey would," he told the *New York Times*. "And in many instances we do what he wouldn't. But we all got infected by that same bug: 'Don't think small. There's no such thing as a small film, only small audiences.' " That's *inspiration*, not mindless cloning.

Like to harness the brain power of experts for ZERO dollars a day? Just ask yourself: *What would ______ do?* In addition to choosing a mentor or a senior statesman in your field, you'll do well by filling in the blank with the name of a famous person whose solution-finding skills you admire—either from the past (say Henry Ford or FDR) or from the present (Bill Gates or Arnold Schwarzenegger perhaps).

Tom Hanks, in fact, once asked Schwarzenegger for his advice about promoting movies. As Hanks tells it, Schwarzenegger told him: "You should always have three things in your head that you want to say about your new movie. And you say those things no matter what you're asked." (And that was *before* Schwarzenegger entered politics.)

If you don't have the ear of Gates or Schwarzenegger, there's no need for concern: Just *imagine* what famous people—faced with your particular challenge—would say or do. Chances are, these imaginary friends will guide you well, helping you to replace old line thinking with the wisdom and vision of outstanding artists, statesmen, and leaders of industry, all of whom will be working for YOU for **FREE**.

Do you have a photo or quote that really speaks to you? Look for pictures or quotes you can keep by your desk to be reminded of their message. Maybe its some "great idea" from Edison or Einstein, or just something you saw on someone's tee shirt one day.

TRUE STORY

Years ago, a friend came over wearing a tee shirt that read: "Progress, not perfection." This message, based on the teachings of Alcoholics Anonymous, sits in a small frame above my desk and saves my life at least once a day. It reminds me to not even *try* for perfection, because the more I try for it, the less I get done. Instead, I look over my work and ask myself: "Is it better now than it was before?"

If it is, I know I'm making progress—even if it is far from perfect.

Writing this book, I've also been guided by the words of Vladimir Nabokov, who opined: "Style and structure are the essence of a book; great ideas are hogwash." (Come over sometime; you'll find it taped to my monitor.) I admit it: My emphasis throughout—and what has kept me going in times of doubt—in addition to "Progress, not perfection"—is that "style and structure" will, for me, win the day. *Oh, sure. It would be great to have a "great idea" now and then, but that has truly not been my goal.* My goal, instead, is to inject all the enthusiasm, panache, and enjoyment that I can, providing both winning solutions AND lots of fun. (*That's right,* fun.)

CHAPTER TAKE-A-WAYS

Harness the brain power of experts for ZERO dollars a day! All you have to do is ask.

- Asking yourself, "What would _____ do?," fill in the blank with the name of a mentor or a senior statesman in your field. Or fill in the blank with the name of a famous person (past or present) whose solution-finding skills you admire. Your choices here should be more than ample. Be careful to exclude, however, anyone who has served more thirty-seven years in prison.

17

Ask STRANGERS *for Help*

I not only use all the brains I have, but all I can borrow.

—Woodrow Wilson

As a teenager, while swimming in the ocean in the Bahamas, I turned to see how far I had swum from shore. To my surprise, I had swum out much further than I had planned. *No need to panic,* I told myself, *I'll just turn around and start swimming back to shore. Little by little, I'll make it back.* And by using a jetty of rocks that extended from the beach as a yardstick, I figured I could easily measure my progress to shore. For all my efforts, though, I might as well have been swimming on a treadmill: I wasn't drowning, but I wasn't making any progress either. Despite my best swimming efforts, all I was doing was holding my place, treading water despite each stroke.

I scanned the horizon for options. About fifty yards off was a small fishing boat with an outboard motor. I swallowed my pride, and called out in a voice so tentative it couldn't be heard across a room, let alone across an ocean, "Help?" No response. Of course no response! I was too *embarrassed* to give my cry for help the urgency and volume the situation demanded. I tried, this time just a bit less softly, "Help!?" No response. Finally, I called out—just loudly enough, I judged, to be heard and no louder—"Help! Help!"

"What'd you say?" one of them called out.

I said "Help!"

"You *joking?*"

"I'm not joking, I'm drowning!"

That sprung them into action. They turned the boat around and made their way over. With their boat now just a few feet away, one of the passengers noted, quite correctly, in fact, "You don't *look* like you're drowning."

"I'm not, really. It's just that I'm not making any progress and I can't keep swimming in place forever."

"Didn't you know about the undertow?"

"Look, are you going to help me here or not!?"

Finally, they helped me aboard and ferried me back to shore.

The moral of the story? *Better a little embarrassed than dead in the water.*

Remember: When you find yourself thinking, I could use some help, don't be embarrassed about asking for a hand. Preferably, find yourself one or more "strangers," or outsiders—people who are likely to approach your problem or situation in some new, unexpected ways.

During the Cold War, when the CIA wanted to learn a few tricks about the art of deception, it turned to magicians for advice. Today, the United States Army seeks the help of "magicians" from Hollywood—like screenwriter David Ayer (who wrote *Training Day*), writer and director John Milius (cowriter of *Apocalypse Now* and writer and director of *Red Dawn*), and Ron Cobb (conceptual set designer for *Star Wars* and *Aliens*). As reported in the *Los Angeles Times,* "The Institute for Creative Technology is the country's only organization that draws on entertainment industry know-how to sharpen military training through futuristic games and simulation. The institute's Hollywood consultants also write story lines for virtual-reality military training videos—plots with swirling suspense and drama that aim to make a soldier's training more compelling."

In 2004, when the Defense Department's Defense Advanced Research Projects Agency (DARPA) wanted to explore unmanned ground vehicles—either as "donkey" units to move supplies and equipment, or as "fully autonomous combat vehicles"—it created the Grand Challenge, a public competition to build and race prototype vehicles from Los Angeles to Las Vegas in March 2004. Thinking of entering one of your kids' radio-controlled cars? Think again. The vehicles can use no external communication other than satellite-based navigation systems; and all equipment must be self-contained and on-board, including whatever is necessary for refueling or recharging.

When the Department of Transportation sought new ideas for managing traffic, it also asked for help from the public, inviting comments on its Web site in the summer of 2002. Among the suggestions:

- Raise gasoline prices to $5 a gallon. (We're almost there.)
- Build "bicycle highways" to carry thousands of cyclists at a time.
- Carpool or pay: During rush hour, impose tolls for drivers without passengers.
- When traffic is jammed up, have emergency personnel drive around the jam up in all-terrain vehicles.

When the California Highway Patrol (CHP) wanted extra help in rescuing child kidnapping victims, it created the Amber Alert system, a modern day "deputizing" program for enlisting the help of private citizens. By preempting radio and television broadcasts and activating electronic roadside signs (with changeable messages), the Amber Alert system gives real-time information to motorists about child abduction cases—though only if the victim "is in imminent danger of serious injury or death." To further assist CHP, the program has been expanded to include notification to the state's 38,000 truckers—either by CB radios or cell phones—so they can watch for vehicles that might be carrying kidnapped children. (A similar "deputizing" program is created whenever a truck has a bumper sticker that reads: "How am I driving?," followed by a 1-800 telephone number.)

When the North America division of General Motors was looking for ways to improve its manufacturing and customer satisfaction, the company turned to DELL COMPUTERS. (After all, in 2002, GM posted profits of $1.7 billion on $187 billion in revenue, while Dell, with a relatively "meager" revenue of $35.4 billion, netted $2.1 billion.) After GM came calling, so did Ford DaimlerChrysler and Toyota.

Designers of the Windstar minivan for Ford have their own brand of advisors, including employees and their spouses who lease Ford vehicles and are asked for their feedback. So when a woman with young children observed that when she opens the doors after a long drive at night her car's dome light wakes her young children up, the Windstar team created an option for having only the floor lighting turn on instead.

When Black & Decker looks for new product ideas, it turns to focus groups, asking ordinary consumers how they use existing products or what tools they feel are "missing" from their lives. In the 1970s, for example, the company discovered that consumers wanted a portable vacuum cleaner for smaller spills. This led Black & Decker to create the hugely successful Dustbuster. In 1994, hearing that consumers wanted both hands free 75 percent of the time they use a flashlight, the company created the flexible *SnakeLight,* a flashlight that can stand by itself and be pointed in any direction, even wrapped around the wearer's neck.

How does Black & Decker stumble onto these innovative discoveries? They ask lots of questions and listen for needs. Mo Siegel, founder of Celestial Seasonings, liked to say:

"Listening to your customers is a way to make a fortune."

Listening to customers can also save you money and broaden your market. As the *Wall Street Journal* reported in 2003: "For years, Barbie dolls sold in Japan looked different from their U.S. counterparts. They had Asian facial features, black hair, and Japanese-inspired fashions. Then [around 2000] Mattel Inc. conducted consumer research around the world and learned something surprising: *The original Barbie, with her yellow hair and blue eyes, played as well in Hong Kong as it did in Hollywood.*" Armed with this newfound information, not only did Mattel save money by not having to market and create nation-specific Barbie merchandise, it allowed the company to be more aggressive abroad.

Whoever your end-users, go to them directly; ask them: "What do *you* think?"

And it doesn't take a lot of money or a major focus group. Jon Bon Jovi, for example, recalls: "We were making demos for what was our third album in Sayreville, N.J.—my hometown—in a little demo studio. . . . It sounds like I was so smart to poll these people. But the truth is that I went around the corner to have a pizza, and a bunch of kids were in there, and they said we know you guys, you made two records . . . So we invited a dozen of them back and their reaction to various songs helped influence the decision making."

My wife and I took a similar "What do *you* think?" approach in searching for the titles for our first two *Shake It!* Books—our "Husband" and "Wife" books. After coming up with what we believed were half a dozen pretty good titles, we sent our list of titles—via e-mail—to more than one hundred married people, asking them to vote for their favorite. The second most popular pair of titles was *How to Be The Perfect Husband (By Wives Who Know)* and *How to Be The Perfect Wife (By Husbands Who Know)*, preferred by nearly 15 percent of those surveyed. The most popular titles—by a whopping *70 percent*—were those that added the word "almost," making the winning titles *How to Be The Almost Perfect Husband (By Wives Who Know)* and *How to Be The Almost Perfect Wife (By Husbands Who Know)*.

Not only did our survey not cost a thing, consumer feedback repeatedly indicates we picked the right titles. "It's the word 'almost'" people tell us, completely unsolicited. "Without that word it wouldn't be believable."

1 + 1 = 3 OR MORE

Strangers are not the only ones who can help. One of the most powerful ways to increase your creative potential is by creating alliances that can multiply your brain power by many times more than the number of people involved. In his classic, *Think and Grow Rich*, Napoleon Hill observes: "No two minds ever come together without, thereby, creating a third, invisible, intangible force which may be likened to a third mind." Describing his "Mastermind" principal, Hill explains that when two or more people coordinate harmoniously, they tap into "the source to which the genius and every great leader turn."

Author and speaker Ed Rigsbee comes to the same conclusion in his book *The Art of Partnering*. Defining partnering as "the process of two or more entities coming together for the purpose of developing synergistic solutions to their challenges," he demonstrates how businesses large or small can profitably partner with suppliers, employees, customers, even *competitors* for synergistic solutions. *(Having partnered with Rigsbee—a so-called competitor—I can tell you he's right. Look. He just got his name in my book.)*

Finally, when asking for help, be clear. What happens when you *don't* communicate clearly? Consider the following TV commercial: We see two men trying to maneuver a sofa through a doorway, each holding up one end of the sofa—one in the hallway, one in the living room. They push, pull, struggle, and strain. Finally, the guy in the hallway says, "I don't think we're ever getting this out of here." To which his startled partner replies, *"Out of here!?!?"*

CHAPTER TAKE-A-WAYS

When you find yourself thinking, *I could use some help,* bring some "strangers" into the mix—people who are likely to approach your problem or situation in new, unexpected ways.

- Whether your market is kids, moms, or any other group of consumers, go to them directly; ask them: "What do *you* think?"
- Consider "deputizing" the public to assist you. (Think "How am I driving?" or Amber Alert).
- Look for a company in a *different* industry that's already successful with something you're struggling to achiever or improve. Then see what you can "borrow" for your own purposes.

Finally . . .

- Ask your *customers* what they think. Then listen very carefully.

18

Never Take YES for an ANSWER

Airplane interior specialist Klaus Brauer confided to the *Wall Street Journal:* "Every time we design a new airplane, we come up with ideas that make us slap ourselves on the forehead and ask, 'Why didn't we think of that before?' " To reduce your forehead-slapping moments, learn not to say, "Yes, that's it!" but, "Yes, that *could* be it." Then go find some more solutions.

Case in point. Starting around 2000, music CD sales went into a slump from which they've yet to recover. Unhappy with the prospect of having to pay $18 or more for a CD, people started buying fewer CDs. They also started burning perfect "clones" of their friends' CDs—creating their own version of "two for one" sales. (Or "three for one" or "four or more for one.") Then things really got out of hand with the introduction of online systems like Napster and peer-to-peer file sharing. Suddenly, people could "share" their music libraries online—not just with friends, but with millions of strangers—without the record companies getting a dime. (Hollywood became concerned as well, fearful that people would soon be illegally downloading whole movies with equal abandon. While this chapter focuses primarily on the music industry, the proposed solutions could certainly be "borrowed" for application to Hollywood.)

The music industry's initial response? The Recording Industry of America Association (RIAA) sued Napster out of business. And the record companies went after consumers directly, threatening fines of up to $150,000 per uploaded song while earning headlines like: "Music Industry Sues Twelve Year Old." (In fact, the industry has already settled hundreds of these lawsuits, for an average settlement of around $3,000.) *Why all the litigation?* To let the public know that the music industry is mad as hell and it's not going to take it anymore. Sadly, this tactic is akin to placing thugs with clubs outside music stores where sales are sluggish. The message? *Since we're not selling much music, if you make matters worse by trying to steal some we will come down on you like a ton of bricks.*

Rather than viewing file sharing as a *crisis,* the industry began to see it as an *opportunity.* (As music legend Duke Ellington put it: "A problem is a chance to do your best.") So instead of asking:

"How can we get people to
<u>stop</u> <u>stealing</u> our music?"

The industry started asking:

"How can we get people to
<u>start</u> <u>buying</u> our music?"

One solution was to try to wean users from *illegal* downloads by offering *legal* alternatives—like Apple's iTunes Music Store—hoping that attractive pricing (99 cents per tune) could make *buying* music as attractive as *stealing* it. Launched in May 2003, iTunes was an immediate hit, getting consumers to *buy,* not steal, more than 300 million songs in less than two years. (Similar services, like RealNetworks' Rhapsody, Yahoo's Musicmatch, and the resurrected *legal* version of Napster are also making a go of it.)

But what about before *iTunes and others could establish themselves as viable business and technological models? Was there anything "in the room" the industry could use to help boost sales?*

Enter Bon Jovi—about six months before the birth of iTunes. Starting in 2002, with the release of its album, *Bounce,* when you purchased one of the group's CDs you got a serial number that was unique to you. You then went to the band's Web site, entered some personal information, and became a registered Bon Jovi Fan Club member. *Who cares?* Their fans care! Because as a registered fan you get:

Band-related online freebies.
Preference in buying concert tickets.
The possibility of climbing on stage with the band.
The opportunity (if you're lucky) to "chat on line" with band members.
And, as they say, lots, lots more!

In other words, said Bon Jovi: *Why STEAL our music when BUYING our music gives you so much more?* Meanwhile, all these "extras" cost Bon Jovi close to ZERO. (Talk about an elegant solution!) Plus, the band's management could now use the data it collected from club members to market the band *directly* to fans long after the album is released. Think tee shirts, posters, and more and more sources of additional revenue.

Still not convinced of the power of "more"? In 2005, Bruce Springsteen, released his latest album, *Devils & Dust,* on the relatively new DualDisc format, giving fans a CD on one side of the disc, a DVD on the other. Why throw in a DVD for just a dollar or two more? Since consumers already perceive DVDs to have a better value proposition, the idea behind DualDiscs is to give consumers a big increase in perceived value at a minimal cost to the record company. In other words, *Let's give consumers a compelling reason to start buying discs again!*

POP QUIZ

You're the head of a major record label. What's your strategy?

(a) Lawsuits.
(b) Selling downloads.
(c) Offering more (DualDiscs, Bon Jovi-like freebies).
(d) All of the above.
(e) Keep searching for MORE solutions.

The correct answer is "e," keep searching for MORE solutions.

Remember: You always want to pose your question as many ways as possible. So instead of simply replacing:

"How can we get people to
stop stealing our music?"

With:

"How can we get people to
start buying our music?"

What if we asked that same question in a *slightly different* way? Like:

"How can we get people to start
paying for our music?"

What's the difference? A lot, as evidenced by the following solutions (or answers) to our only slightly different question: "How can we get people to start **paying** for our music?"

- Borrow the video rental model and encourage consumers to rent their music. Not by renting something physical, like a CD, but by subscribing to an online service, like Rhapsody or EMusic. A *music*-renting *business*? If that seems strange (even "absurd"), consider this: When George Atkinson opened the first video rental store in 1979, the concept quickly caught on with the public. The movie studios, however, were fearful that the *renting* of videos would compromise their original plan: to sell a limited quantity of high-priced videos to serious, affluent collectors. But when the rental business became more lucrative than the selling model ever was, the studios realized it was a *Good idea!* after all. Meanwhile, if the public reacts the way it did to the renting of videos, it's conceivable that the renting of music via the Internet could supplant the CD business, reducing the industry's cost to manufacture and ship its product to almost ZERO.
- License your music for cell-phone ring tones (currently a $2.2 billion business worldwide).
- Instead of a *lawsuit* or *legal*-downloading approach, take a *taxing* approach. William Fisher, a Harvard University law professor and director of the Berkman Center for Internet and Society, recommends a 15 percent tax on the purchase of "devices used for storing and copying music and movies—like CD burners, MP3 players, and blank CDs."

  A *revolutionary approach?* Hardly. In the 1920s and 1930s, the growing popularity of radio posed a similar problem. *How could music companies and publishers get compensated equitably for the music radio stations were broadcasting to listeners for free?* The solution? Radio stations agreed to set up a monitoring system and pay the record companies for the music they were playing. The payments were *estimates,* with larger payments going to more popular songs, and so on. (Fisher's idea is a good example of "borrowing"—in this case "borrowing" a solution from the early days of radio and applying it in response to the pirating of music online.)

According to Fisher, had such a system been in effect in 2004, the funds raised would have been about $2.5 billion—roughly the same amount the recording industry and Hollywood estimates it loses each year to online piracy.

And, for a "radical" yet common-sense solution, how about this?

- *Lower the price of CDs.* Make less money per disc, but sell more of them—something the industry has very much started to do.

Meanwhile, what if we tried an "opposites" approach to the above solution?

- Instead of lowering the price of CDs, what if the industry RAISED their price? *Absurd,* you say? Think again. Because record companies are doing just that. (Sort of.) Trying to attract hard-core fans (who are often willing to shell out more money), the industry now sells higher-priced "packages" in addition to basic CDs. If you're a U2 fan, for example, you can get their *How to Dismantle an Atomic Bomb* CD three different ways: CD only, "Deluxe Edition" (CD + DVD), and "Collector's Edition" (CD + DVD + fifty-page hardcover book). Similarly, Eminem fans can go for broke with the "Limited Collector's Edition" of *Encore* (CD + bonus CD + photos + lyrics + cell-phone ring tone).

  Today, a no-frills CD has a list price of about $14; "bonus packages" significantly more—from about $23 to $40. And while no one expects them to sell through the roof (they generally account for 10 to 20 percent of an album's volume), their profit margin is often higher than for CDs alone. The formula is simple: *Charge 'em more, give 'em more—costing you comparatively less—and wind up profiting a whole lot more.*

Chances are, one or more of the above solutions have already made you think, "Yes, that's it!" But let's keep going a bit: Remember McCabe, the college professor? He suggested that when dealing with students who plagiarize, instead of asking:

"How do we catch them <u>after</u> they've cheated?"

We should be asking:

"How do we catch them <u>before</u> they've cheated?"

How do you catch music "pirates" before *they've cheated?*

- Have music companies—in conjunction with schools—teach *ethics,* including the concept that it's wrong to steal.
- Or how about an "Aikido" approach? What if the industry took teen "pirates" and hired them as paid consultants? *Paying* teenagers—*the offenders themselves—to be consultants?* If law enforcement agencies like the FBI can hire former computer hackers, why not? Have the industry speak with the "pirates" directly, asking them questions like:

What do YOU think we should do to stop illegal downloading?

What do YOU think we should do to sell or rent more music?

In other words . . .

What would work for <u>YOU</u>?

POP QUIZ

In place of the industry's initial response (lawsuits), you've just been presented with more than half a dozen solid alternatives. Now imagine you're a high-priced consultant charged with coming up with even *more* solutions. In an attempt to reduce your future forehead-slapping moments to zero, how many more "Yes, that *could* be it" solutions can you think of?

If you'd like, you can e-mail your solutions to me at joel@shakethatbrain.com. I'll post them on my Web site and send you a link to "Readers Solutions." (Special Note: If you've got a crazy or "absurd" idea, please be sure to send it along.)

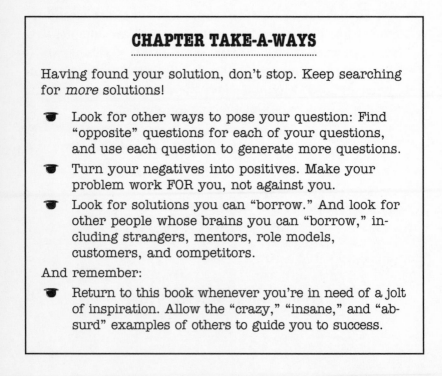

CHAPTER TAKE-A-WAYS

Having found your solution, don't stop. Keep searching for *more* solutions!

- Look for other ways to pose your question: Find "opposite" questions for each of your questions, and use each question to generate more questions.
- Turn your negatives into positives. Make your problem work FOR you, not against you.
- Look for solutions you can "borrow." And look for other people whose brains you can "borrow," including strangers, mentors, role models, customers, and competitors.

And remember:

- Return to this book whenever you're in need of a jolt of inspiration. Allow the "crazy," "insane," and "absurd" examples of others to guide you to success.

19

WRITE It Down!

Years ago, while working as a freelance writer, someone at a party asked me, "Why can't I write?" This was not an easy question, and I soon found myself going on and on about not much at all. Finally, after fifteen minutes or so of blathering like an idiot, I heard myself say, "Look, if you can talk, you can write." Knowing a good line when I hear one, I immediately grabbed a cocktail napkin and wrote it down. Had I not put those words to paper, not only would I have forgotten them by morning, I never would have written my first book ever, *If You Can Talk, You Can Write.*

Got an idea or a great solution? Write it down before it gets away!

Everyone gets great ideas. EVERYONE. Something just POPS into your head, or you're having a conversation when a really COOL IDEA falls from your mouth (or from someone else's mouth).

Unfortunately, few of us make a habit of jotting down our thoughts, making a habit, instead, of saying to ourselves: *I'll remember that,* or *I'll write it down when I get a chance.* Ever had a great idea in the shower, then stepped out a few minutes later only to curse yourself for not jotting it down the MOMENT it came to you? I'll bet you have.

Einstein claimed he got his best ideas while shaving. Yet, I suspect, he was smart enough to JOT THEM DOWN before they vanished down the drain.

Got an idea while taking a shower? Be prepared with a Plexiglas notepad attached to your shower wall with suction cups. Or brave the cold, step outside, and jot it down with that pen and pad you so wisely left out on the vanity. Scrawl it on the mirror if you have to—anything to make sure you grab it while you can. As Nolan Bushnell, Founder of Atari and Chuck E. Cheese, puts it: "Everyone who's ever taken a shower has an idea. It's the person who gets out of the shower, dries off and does something about it who makes a difference."

Got an idea while driving down the road? Unless someone else is doing the driving, pull off to the shoulder before you write it down. Or, once you pull over, dial your voicemail and leave yourself a message explaining it all. Do NOT attempt to write down your thoughts while piloting your SUV. It's not safe for you, or for the other guy. As James Dean famously ad-libbed in a public service announcement about drinking and driving: "The life you save may be mine."

Got an idea just as you're drifting off to sleep, or just at the moment you start to wake? Quick. Write it down on your bedside pad—before you take a shower, make the coffee, or just plain forget it as you get on with your day. Later, you'll find the time to review that "great idea" you so wisely put to paper. You'll discover that it's great, pretty good, so-so, or just plain lousy. Though from time to time you may just conclude: "This idea is worth a million bucks! All I have to do now . . . is get to work on it."

I keep a notebook in my pocket at all time[s], and I really do listen to what people say, even when we're out in a club at 3 a.m. and someone's passing on an idea in a drunken slur. Good ideas come from people everywhere, not in the boardroom.

—Richard Branson, Chairman, the Virgin Group

More than 200 companies "involved in," according to Virgin's Web site, "planes, trains, finance, soft drinks, music, mobile phones, holidays, cars, wines, publishing, bridal wear . . . the lot!"

READER BEWARE: Censorship often begins at home, when you suddenly get a "great idea!" then—just as suddenly—decide it's not such a "great idea" after all. In fact, *It stinks.* (Samuel Goldwyn once remarked, "I had a monumental idea this morning, but I didn't like it.") Got an idea? Jot it down. And maybe—just maybe—you'll become rich and famous for going ahead with that "monumental idea." As Mary Kay Ash so brilliantly put it: "Ideas are a dime a dozen. People who implement them are priceless."

CHAPTER TAKE-A-WAYS

What's the first thing to do soon as you get a great idea? Write it down.

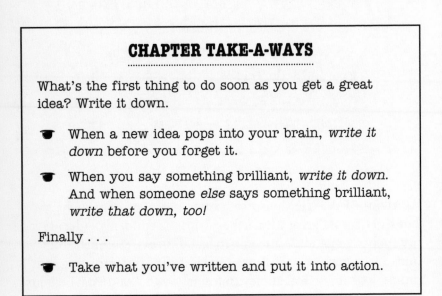

- When a new idea pops into your brain, *write it down* before you forget it.
- When you say something brilliant, *write it down.* And when someone *else* says something brilliant, *write that down, too!*

Finally . . .

- Take what you've written and put it into action.

20

Walk AWAY from It

Push away from your desk. Take a walk. Take your dog for a walk. *Solvitur ambulando.* ("It is solved by walking.")

When Google cofounder Larry Page was asked where he did his best thinking he replied: "Rollerblading; in Hawaii; when I'm hanging out and chatting with friends. Anywhere but the office." Today, the problem of having our office environment stifle our creativity is greater than ever because even when we *leave* the office, we often take much of it with us. Whether it's your cell phone, laptop, or BlackBerry that's got you by the wireless hairs, what's at risk is the free-floating, creative, discovery-inducing YOU. The solution? Schedule yourself an appointment to:

Unplug, discharge, stop, and smell the roses.

You'll recharge your creative batteries and get yourself a fresh point of view. You'll also come up . . . with better solutions.

Mathematician Henri Poincaré (1854–1912) was a strong believer in the benefits of taking a break now and then. He wrote: "Disgusted with my failure [to solve some mathematical questions], I went to spend a few days at the seaside, and thought of something else. One morning, walking on the bluff, the idea came to me, with . . . brevity, suddenness and immediate certainty, that the arithmetic transformations of indeterminate ternary quadratic forms were identical with those of non-Euclidean geometry." (But you probably already knew that.)

Poincaré believed that travel allowed him to "forget" his mathematical work. He recalls, on another occasion, having "entered an omnibus to go some place or other. At the moment when I put my foot on the step the idea came to me, without anything in my former thoughts seeming to have paved the way for it."

Take a break, take a shower, take a bus if you have to. "Taking a break," says composer David Byrne, ". . . gives you stuff to draw on, gives you inspiration." "You go back to it," adds novelist John Irving, "and you suddenly see something that if you'd been rushing and pushing you wouldn't have seen it."

Consider the story of Archimedes and the King of Syracuse: The king was presented with a beautiful crown made of solid gold—or so he'd been told. The king suspected the gold had been mixed with silver, thereby reducing the cost to its makers (and its value to the king). For help, he turned to Archimedes, a noted mathematician and scientist. "Archimedes, *you* figure it out!" He knew how much a certain volume of gold should weigh. Say a gold bar of certain dimensions. *But how,* he wondered, *do you figure out the volume of an irregular shape like the crown without having to melt it down?* Archimedes was stumped. Really stumped. Then one day, tired and frustrated from having gotten nowhere with his problem, he thought he'd soak away his troubles in a nice hot bath. He filled it up, lowered himself in, and, noticing how the tub overflowed from the added volume of his body, the solution to his problem suddenly appeared: An object—whether it be a body or a crown—displaces a volume of water equal to its own. "Eureka!"

For weeks, writer Nicholas Meyer struggled to find a way to adapt Philip Roth's novel *The Human Stain* into a screenplay. Finally, he decided to admit defeat. "It was a big weight off my shoulders," he confessed to the *New York Times*. "Then out of the blue, inspiration struck. I was sitting there in the bathtub, staring at my toes getting wrinkled, and I was not thinking about this at all . . . when suddenly, out of nowhere, like tumblers clicking successively into place on a safe: Act I, Act II, Act III. Don't know why, don't know where it came from." Three months later, Meyer completed his first draft screenplay.

TRUE STORY

Back when I was a fledgling writer working out of my apartment in New York, if I'd get stumped at the keyboard, I'd move to the terrace, leaving my typewriter behind and settling down in my Adirondack chair for a much-needed change of scenery.

Over the years, I discovered that if I went out to the terrace with a pad and pencil, I hardly ever came up with a solution to whatever problem I'd gone there to solve; but if I went out to the terrace WITHOUT a pad and pencil, I'd invariably find my solution. Then I'd race back inside and write it down before I forgot it. It was as if I had tricked my mind into thinking I was on vacation. Once on "vacation," it seems, my mind could unwind enough to reveal my solutions.

Let your problems go for a while . . . and the answer may just come to you. Remember: *Solvitur ambulando.* ("It is solved by walking.") It is also solved by:

Going to the beach
Taking a bike ride
Taking a bus
Taking a shower
Shaving
Rollerblading
Hanging out
Chatting with friends
Playing Frisbee (how Feynman got one of his best ideas)
Taking a nap
Goofing off
Goofing around
Going for a round of golf
Puttering around the garage
Playing with Silly Putty
(You get the idea.)

CHAPTER TAKE-A-WAYS

Struggling for a solution that just won't come? Stop and smell the roses. You'll recharge your creative batteries and get yourself a fresh point of view.

Solvitur ambulando.

(It is solved by walking.)

Part Three

SELLING

– Or –

How to Avoid Having to Scream, "Why doesn't anyone get this great idea that could just win a Nobel Prize!?"

No matter how wonderful your great new idea, be prepared for opposition—from bosses, coworkers, spouses, in-laws, and more. To overcome this opposition you'll need to learn the first rule of trailblazing—selling. Because in order to succeed, you will have to sell. The trick is knowing how to do it.

21

Sell It to YOU

Your first sales job is communicating the value of Project X to the captain of your team—you. Otherwise, you face an uphill battle, asking yourself, *If I can't sell me, how can I sell anyone else?* What's required is developing an unwavering belief in the value of your project. As a role model consider Mary Kay Ash, founder of May Kay Cosmetics, who said: "We only have 10 percent of the market, and that means that 90 percent of the women are buying the wrong cosmetics."

What happens when you fail to develop "an unwavering belief in the value of your project?" You lose.

In 1874, demonstrations by inventor Elisha Gray prompted the *New York Times* to write that telegraph operators would soon "transmit the sound of their own voices over the wire, and talk with one another instead of telegraphing." The *Times,* however, was in the minority: Neither private industry, Gray's business partners, or Gray's own patent attorney saw a profitable future for his findings. Bowed by negativity, Gray gave up, called it quits. Yet one year later, he happened upon a discovery—the "missing ingredient"—that would make his telephone idea viable after all. Then emotions took over: Gray's self-doubt caused him to wait more than two months before he attempted to patent his idea. As a result, Gray's application got to the patent office just two hours *later* than a similar set of drawings—created and signed by Alexander Graham Bell.

Once again, for emphasis:

What happens when you fail to develop "an unwavering belief in the value of your project?"

You lose.

22

Sell It to OTHERS

In addition to being your own best cheerleader, you'll need to communicate your vision to others. In 1979, while working to drum up support for his Macintosh project at Apple, Jeff Raskin met with serious opposition. With Apple II's comfortably selling at the rate of 10,000 a year, management had no interest in a computer that did not have Apple II compatibility. That's why, recalled Raskin, he "wrote forward-looking white papers like 'Computers by the Millions' so that management could see what the computing world would be like in the coming decade."

When "selling" your idea to others, present it in a way that is clear, concise, and compelling. For example: "Computers by the Millions" at a time when computers were selling by the *thousands.*

TRUE STORY

Each year, the National Academy of Engineering awards the Charles Stark Draper Prize to an engineer who "has significantly impacted society by improving the quality of life." In 1997, the award committee decided to award the prize to Professor Vladimir Haensel for his work in developing "platinum reforming"—a chemical process for making lead-free gasoline, among other uses. But the committee was concerned (appropriately) that it was going to have a tough time getting publicity for platinum reforming. They scratched their heads, shook their brains, and—finally—came up with a sound byte that, they agreed, was "both accurate and accessible." They told the media that without this thing called platinum reforming: "All of our IQ's would have been 10 points lower, on account of all the lead in the air."

Now imagine the following (completely hypothetical): When Professor Haensel was looking for research money for his work, suppose he had gone to a funding group and said: "Ladies and gentlemen: If you don't fund this research, everyone in this room is going to lose 10 points from their IQ."

Clear and concise? Yes.

Compelling? You betcha!

23

BUILD It

Whether it's a product or service, or a better, faster, or cheaper way of doing X, build a prototype to prove your case—and to learn what needs to be retooled or revised.

Build a prototype? Do you have any idea what that would cost!?

Chances are, a lot less than you think.

In 1980, Steve Jobs asked Dean Hovey, the young head of a start-up industrial design firm, to design a computer mouse. At the time, the only one on the market was an unreliable commercial model for $400 from IBM. Not only was Jobs asking for a superior, consumer-oriented mouse, he wanted one that could be mass produced for $10 to $35.

Hovey-Kelley, hungry to make a name for itself, went to work with limited resources, knowing they'd have to think *creatively* to get the job done, from using what was "in the room"—borrowing parts from Hovey's home refrigerator—to budget shopping at the local Walgreens (what Hovey called "the mouse parts store") for items like a bottle of Ban Roll-On deodorant for the mouse ball and a plastic butter dish for the housing. In the end, the Apple mouse put Hovey-Kelley on the map. Big time.

Jobs's assignment was to deliver a prototype; it was not something "optional." But the lesson to be learned applies nonetheless: Building that prototype can be accomplished for a lot less money than you'd imagine.

When *Shake It!* Books launched our *Almost Perfect Husband* and *Almost Perfect Wife* books, we decided to create prototypes so our sales representatives could show them to buyers. We printed the pages off our home computer, borrowed an arm and lever paper cutter to chop them down to size (4″ × 6″) and, to keep the pages together, created what's called a "perfect binding" with a five-dollar jar of padding glue and my index finger. For covers, which had to be made in two pieces to fit on an 8½″ × 11″ sheet of paper, we had our local copy shop make colored copies on glossy stock for an up-charge of 20 cents each. Then we glued the covers together and secured them to the binding with a final swipe of my finger. Our total out-of-pocket cost for twenty prototype books (including paper) was about $32.

Rather than making their sales pitch relying on sample covers and a one-page description, our reps now had actual books they could place in the hands of buyers—helping to generate initial orders that, according to our distributor, were the largest they had seen in ten years in business. (Within the next few years, we sold more than 250,000 copies combined, making each book a best seller two-and-a-half times over.)

How much did our prototypes help? A whole lot more than $32 worth. And because we had prototypes, we received feedback that contributed in no small measure to the success of our finished books. As plastics tycoon Baekeland advised: "Commit your blunders on a small scale, and make your profits on a large scale." (And let me tell you—when you're financing a first printing of 40,000 books with your credit card, you cannot afford to blunder your way.)

24

Demonstrate Its Value with P.O.P.

Use your prototype to "prove" your case—to demonstrate to potential allies and buyers why this "really-cool-new-idea" is, in fact, a *profit-making, cost-reducing, time-saving, or life-enhancing solution they just can't live without.* The issue is proof:

WHAT CAN YOU DO TO PROVE THE VALUE OF YOUR NEW PRODUCT, SERVICE, OR THEORY?

Remember Hawkins's "opposite" question: "How do I teach the **users** of [the Palm Pilot] **one** handwriting style?" First, he worked to create this new writing language that would be *close* to printed English but also have some major differences, allowing each letter of the alphabet to be written in a single stroke. (The letter A for example, would be written without the horizontal line; the letter F without the lower horizontal line.) Next, he worked to hone and perfect his symbols through a series of incarnations, or *prototypes,* until he developed "an unwavering belief" in his new written language—as well as his ability to easily write it himself.

Finally, Hawkins demonstrated to his team just how easy it was to work with these new symbols. Their response was emphatic: *Ask people to learn a whole new way to write!? That's absurd!*

But Hawkins pressed on, asking them to try learning and practicing it themselves. And within a few days, they each became Graffiti converts. Learning was quick, painless, even FUN.

Through an offer of proof—*Try it, you'll like it*—Hawkins turned a team of skeptics into wide-eyed believers. Such is the power of a compelling proof. For shorthand, think:

P.O.P.
(The Power of Proof)

For example . . .

The Proof about Tanning

Living in Southern California, I see lots of people with really good tans—only tans aren't good for you. So why do so many people go without sunscreens or protective clothing? (1) Because tans look good, and (2) because many people have not been "sold" on the need for sun protection.

To see how beachgoers could be better convinced to use sunscreen and avoid tanning, researchers at University of California at San Diego (UCSD) discovered that handing out brochures on photoaging and sun protection wasn't enough; but when they employed a UV ray-filtered instant camera to reveal the underlying damage in a person's facial skin—Wow! Those who saw photos of themselves—with visible PROOF of their existing sun damage—pretty much stopped sunbathing and were more likely to protect themselves from the sun when out and about.

The Proof about Glare

Edwin Land had a plan to communicate the value of his own sun-related innovation not by using photos or charts, but by showing it in action to executives from the American Optical Company. Land arranged for a meeting in a hotel in Boston. When the executives entered the room they were met by glaring sunlight from the western exposure. Land apologized for the glare, adding, "I imagine you can't even see the fish." Then he gave each of them a sample of polarizer film and told them to hold it up to their eyes. Immediately, they saw six goldfish swimming in a bowl on the window ledge, which is how Edwin Land convinced the American Optical Company to make its sunglasses with Polaroid lenses.

The Proof about Those O-Rings

Remember Feynman's ice water demonstration? Removing his C-clamp and O-ring rubber sample from the ice water, he neatly demonstrated the rubber's lack of resilience at colder temperatures by loosening the clamp and showing how the rubber did *not* instantly return to its original size. Now. Compare Feynman's low-tech demonstration to a series of PowerPoint slides. Which presentation would you prefer? (*Wait, Joel, that's not fair. You're trying to push us into an Either/Or choice.*) Okay, how about this question: Do you think Feynman's "stunt" was a powerful offer of proof? *You bet it was.*

In fact, Feynman's "elegant solution"—devised from such basic materials that the public could easily grok it—earned him press around the world. People also appreciated the sideshow aspect of his stunt. *Here's a roomful of scientists trying to figure out what went wrong with a multimillion dollar rocket and this guy proves his theory with a glass of ice water!*

25

Get SUPPORT for It

Today, it's hard to imagine a world without Post-it Notes; yet when corporate scientist Art Fry proposed the idea at 3M no one could imagine a world *with* Post-it Notes. So Fry went about building support for his "repositionable notes" by *demonstrating* their value: He gave out samples to secretaries and other influential people and kept careful track of their use. As soon as someone used up their samples, new supplies were delivered fast. It didn't take long for people to depend on these handy notes. "They had become," says Fry, "addicted to them."

Fry's strategy, much like Hawkins's, was simple and direct—*Try it, you'll like it*—a compelling form of P.O.P. (the Power of Proof).

You can also recruit allies by *asking* for allies. Legendary Speaker of the House of Representatives Tip O'Neil often told the story of being surprised that his next-door neighbor hadn't voted for him. When he asked her why, she replied, "Because you never asked me." *Looking for support?* Demonstrate the value of your new idea and tell people-who-can-help-you you need their support.

26

Call It Something CATCHY

In the following pairs, which name, or title, appeals more to you?

Patagonian Tooth Fish
(its original name)

or

Chilean Sea Bass
(it's new name)

The Modified Carbohydrate Diet
(its original title)

or

The South Beach Diet
(its final title)

Repositionable Notes

or

Post-it Notes

What's in a name? *Everything.*

There were months of discussions of what to call themselves.

"Owl Stretching Time"

"Bum, Wackett, Buzzard, Stubble, and Boot"

"Gwen Dibley's Flying Circus"

Finally, recalls Terry Jones, someone said "'How about something slimy, like a python?' And then Eric [Idle] said something about a seedy music hall agent named Monty. And we all said, 'That's it!'"

And that's how six zany lads came to be known as "Monty Python's Flying Circus."

27

Be PERSISTENT

Selling your idea will take persistence. Lots of it. In fact, when a prospect says No, *smart* sales people don't hear "No"—they hear, "Not yet."

That's a "Not yet." . . .
That's a "Not yet." . . .
That's a "Not yet." . . .
That's a "Yes!"

Starting in 1967, engineer and inventor Allen Breed tried to sell air bags to Detroit automakers. But the Big Three wanted no part of this new and expensive technology, and they kept saying No, until an act of Congress, mandating air bags for new cars, forced the industry's hand in 1984. By 1995, nearly thirty years after Breed's first rejection, Breed Technologies had sold 23 million air-bag sensors for a net profit of $110 million. Looking back on the old days, Breed recalled: "We lost track of how many times we heard No."

In 1981, when the advertising agency DDB Needham lost the McDonald's account to competitor Leo Burnett, Chairman and CEO Keith Reinhard refused to admit defeat. For fifteen years he kept sending McDonald's new campaigns his agency had created for the fast-food giant. Finally, in 1997 McDonald's decided it was time to split from Leo Burnett and wound up going—big surprise—back to Needham. The value of the account? $385 million a year.

"I lose most of the time," says Ted Turner. "For me, losing is just learning how to win."

28

KEEP Having FUN with It

Though stated more than once, it still bears repeating: That "great idea" of yours will be met with varying degrees of skepticism, opposition, ridicule, scorn, and outright hostility. While you can't control people's initial reactions—there will be opposition—you can control your *attitude.* The solution? *Keep having fun with it!*

So treat it like a game—because it *is* a game: the "Selling My Idea" game. To win, you'll need to encourage others to follow in your path: to *Shake That Brain! . . . Question Assumptions* . . . and, finally, get everyone who's anyone to stand up and cheer:

"This is a great and wonderful idea!"

Meanwhile, until everyone becomes as enlightened as you, remember: Some people hear "No," others, "Not yet."

That's a "Not yet." . . .
That's a "Not yet." . . .
That's a "Not yet." . . .

That's a "Not yet." . . .
That's a "Not yet." . . .
That's a "Not yet." . . .
That's a "Not yet." . . .
That's a "Not yet." . . .
That's a "Not yet." . . .
That's a "Not yet." . . .
That's a "Not yet." . . .
That's a "Not yet." . . .
That's a "Not yet." . . .
That's a "Not yet." . . .
That's a "Not yet." . . .
That's a "Not yet." . . .
That's a "Not yet." . . .
(Strike seventeen and I'm still up at bat.)
That's a "Not yet." . . .
That's a "Not yet." . . .
That's a "Yes!"

That said, allow me to conclude this book with the same words I use to close each *Shake That Brain!* performance:

Congratulations, today is your day!
You're off to solve problems starting this very day.
Faced with a problem, you know what to do:
Face it head on, no "Boo hoo!" for you!
No shouting, no pouting, no saying, "I can't."
"I can't" is for sissies with ants in their pants.
Remember our mantra, repeat after me:
Shake That Brain, baby!
Set yourself free!

So now I bid a fond adieu
As I remind each one of you:

I said what I meant
And I meant what I said:
"Whether it ends with a fizz or a wow,
When it's all over I'm takin' my bow."

[He tips his derby, takes a bow, and exits.]

Notes

But first, a note about the Notes.

While I have made every attempt to provide the source of most quoted material in this book (citing either the book or article where the words originally appeared), certain quotes (mostly those presented in boxes or larger type) will not be found in this Notes section. Mostly, these are quotes that have been passed down through the ages (or at least the years). Often lacking a precise source, their accuracy may be anywhere on the map—from completely factual to totally apocryphal.

For example, Schopenhauer is said to have said: "All truth passes through three stages. First, it is ridiculed. Second, it is violently opposed. Third, it is accepted as self-evident." Now go try to find the *source* of that quote. *Where, exactly, did he say or write exactly that?*

While it's believable he may have said such a thing (even if he didn't), for our purposes *it simply doesn't matter*. What's important is not whether these statements are one hundred percent factually correct (I'll leave that to the academicians); what's important is the wisdom, or truths, they serve to reveal.

That said, you now have two choices (at least):

1. Ignore those quotes presented in boxes or larger type, knowing they would fail to pass muster with a Ph.D. review committee.

2. Go with the flow—confident, for example, that even if Mark Twain (or Samuel Clemens) didn't actually say or write, "Everyone complains about the weather, but no one does anything about it," the truth of that statement remains unassailable.

"Truth is tough," Twain is also credited with saying. "It will not break, like a bubble, at a touch; nay, you may kick it about all day, like a football, and it will be round and full at evening."

That said, let the kicking begin!

page 8 "If you've got an innovative idea and the majority does not pooh-pooh it, then the odds are you must not have a very good idea." From *They Made America*, by Harold Evans (Little Brown, 2004).

page 9 "My wife thought I was NUTS. She thought I was following in my father's footsteps . . . [Someone who was] always coming up with spectacular, impractical ideas." From "The Next Small Thing," by Pat Dillon, *Fast Company*, June 1998.

"If you're going to innovate. . . . You have to keep fighting the battles." From "Voices of Innovation: Jeff Hawkins," *BusinessWeek*, October 11, 2004.

page 9 "Everyone thought I was INSANE. From my parents to my art dealer friends to my present-day wife, everyone told me, 'This is the stupidest thing you'll every do.' " From "Eli Wilner's Job: Putting the Frame in the Picture," by John Strausbaugh, *New York Times*, January 4, 2004.

page 10 "Nobody believed it could be done. Yet it was so obvious . . . . Developing a compiler was a logical move; but in matters like this, you don't run against logic—you run against people who can't change their minds." From *Mothers of Invention*, by Ethlie Ann Vare and Greg Ptacek (William Morrow & Co., 1988).

page 11 "Design is a funny word. . . . You have to really grok what it's all about." From *iCon Steve Jobs: The Greatest Second Act in the History of Business*, by Jeffrey S. Young and William L. Simon (Wiley, 2005).

page 11 Forrest Ackerman recalls "driving around with his wife when he heard someone on the radio say 'hi-fi' " leading him to come up with the expression "sci-fi," to which his wife responded, "Forget it, Forrie. It will never catch on." From "Welcome to His Planet," by Hilary E. MacGregor, *Los Angeles Times,* January 6, 2003.

page 12 "Once, after I had given a lecture at a conference, a fellow scientist told me: 'I just want you to remember one thing. You can always recognize the pioneers by the number of arrows in their back.' " From "Perriconology," by Alex Witchel, *New York Times*, February 6, 2005.

page 15 "You're all by yourself in what feels like the middle of the ocean. You've gotten caught in the impact zone. . . . But of course, you can't give in to that." From personal correspondence with the author.

page 19 "Creativity is allowing yourself to make mistakes. Art is knowing which ones to keep." From *The Dilbert Principle* by Scott Adams (HarperCollins Publishers, 1996).

page 22 "The only way you learn what works is to learn what doesn't work." From "QuarkXPress Grew Out of Shy Guy's Love of Solitude; Now He's a Huge Philanthropist," by Jim Hopkins, *USA Today*, August 15, 2001.

page 23 "You never know when you're going to fail. That's just part of succeeding—failing. And it's not that big of a deal. It's something to laugh about. You can pick yourself up and go on tomorrow. That's the beauty of it. That's how you succeed." Quoted in *Wynton Marsalis: Trumpet Genius*, by Leslie Gourse (Franklin Watts, 2000).

page 28 "The most creative people I know . . . [refuse] to do anything they don't want to do. . . . 'I have worked every minute of my life,' creative people say. 'And I never did a lick of work in my life.' Both statements are true." Quoted in "They Have a Better Idea . . . Do You?" by Anna Muoio, *Fast Company*, August/September 1997.

page 28 "The idea is to die young as late as possible." Cited by Mihaly Csikszentmihalyi in "They Have a Better Idea . . . Do You?" by Anna Muoio, *Fast Company*, August/September 1997.

page 31 "If you're having fun, you're more likely to be productive. . . . I think we ought to be doing something more fun, something more challenging." From "The Man from Wild Blue Yonder," by Preston Lerner, *Los Angeles Times* magazine, November 21, 1999.

page 31 "He's like a kid in a candy store. He's having more fun than he ever has." From "Entrepreneur of the Year," by David H. Freedman, *Inc.*, January 2005.

page 32 ". . . fun is a basic human need." From "How I Did It: Mike Veeck," by Alan Schwarz, *Inc.*, April 2005.

"Our philosophy begins and ends with the notion that fun is good. . . . We enjoy what we do, and that rubs off on our customers, who leave our ballparks not only entertained but feeling good about themselves and our product." From *Fun Is Good*, by Mike Veeck and Pete Williams (Rodale, 2005).

". . . understood people and that when they had fun, they would spend money." From "How I Did It: Mike Veeck," by Alan Schwarz, *Inc.*, April 2005.

page 34 "If the chairman's having fun, it's easier for everyone else. And if it's fun, you're going to keep going until you drop." From "26 Most Fascinating Entrepreneurs," by Michael S. Hopkins, *Inc.*, April 2005.

page 46 "The preferences about basements were probably there for years, but we never bothered to ask." From "Surprise! A Home

Builder (Finally) Surveys Buyers," by Stacy Kravetz, *Wall Street Journal*, February 11, 1998.

page 48 "Creative people . . . are as curious, engaged, and innocent as children. . . . looking at the world through an ever-changing lens." From "They Have a Better Idea . . . Do You?" by Anna Muoio, *Fast Company*, August/September 1997.

page 62 "If you are able to state a problem—any problem—and if it is important enough, then the problem can be solved." From *Insisting on the Impossible*, by Victor K. McElheny (Perseus Books, 1998).

page 65 ". . . no safety advantage for using a hands-free vs. a hand-held phone. It's conversation that drives this effect. When you're talking, you're impaired." From "The Distraction Factor" *Consumer Reports*, February 2002.

page 70 ". . . more efforts need to go into teaching students not to cheat . . ." From "College Plagiarists Get Caught in the Web," by Jeff Gotlieb, *Los Angeles Times*, January 11, 2000.

page 71 "If you look at the many commercial term paper sites on the internet, you will find that there are large numbers of papers for only a small number of topics. . . . If professors were more creative and less repetitive in their teaching, [the] market for one-size-fits-all term papers would not work as well." From a letter to the editor, "Cheaters on Campus," by Wolfram Latsch, *New York Times*, November 9, 2002.

page 71 "A return is not a return—it's an opportunity." From *Selling with Honor*, by Lawrence Kohn and Joel Saltzman (Berkley Publishing Group, 1997).

pages 76–77 "[T]he cancer establishment's focus remains fixed on damage control—screening, diagnosis, treatment, and related basic research—rather than on preventing cancer in the first place. . . . Focusing on prevention instead would not only save lives: It would save dollars." From "An Ounce of Prevention," by Samuel S. Epstein, M.D., and Quentin D. Young, M.D., *Los Angeles Times*, August 31, 2003.

page 81 "An employer can refuse to hire anyone for any reason as long as it is not an unlawful reason. . . . In fact, if policies against hiring smokers or overweight people cause people to stop smoking or get on the treadmill in order to get a job, it could be seen as a good thing." From Nick Connon, personal correspondence.

pages 81–82 "We told them they had a choice. . . . We just say you can't smoke and work here." From "Kick the Habit—or Get Kicked Off Job," by Kathy Barks Hoffman, *Chicago Tribune*, February 9, 2005.

page 86 "The very essence of the creative is its novelty, and hence we have no standard by which to judge it." From *On Becoming a Person: A Therapist's View of Psychotherapy*, by Carl R. Rogers (Houghton Mifflin, 1961).

page 86 "For two hours . . . you could only contribute to the idea, and that meant that all negatives were out." From *Chuck Amuck: The Life and Times of an Animated Cartoonist*, by Chuck Jones (Farrar, Straus and Giroux, 1989).

page 86 ". . . agree with any premise, no matter how absurd, and then follow and amplify it, working with fellow players who will 'yes, and' any idea of yours." From "A Man of Infinite Jest," by Bob Harris, *Mother Jones*, March 9, 1999.

page 90 Likening Playboy on the radio to "a driver's manual in Braille." From "Without Pictures Playboy Still Draws," by Steve Carney, *Los Angeles Times*, September 5, 2003.

page 90 Museum of Sex (MOSEX) aims "to preserve and present the history, evolution, and cultural significance of human sexuality." From "MOSEX opens door—earth doesn't move," by Damien Cave, online at Salon.com, October 11, 2002.

page 91 "To opposing parties and their counsel, I pledge fairness, integrity, and civility, not only in court, but also in all written and oral communications." From "The 2003 Lawyer's Oath," South Carolina Bar.

page 91 Lawyer cited for "insulting, threatening, and demeaning" witnesses during depositions, including having said to one witness: "You are a mean-spirited, vicious witch and I don't like your face and I don't like your voice." From an editorial, *Chicago Tribune*, March 8, 2005.

pages 91–92 Featuring parachutes "as big as a house," BRS hopes to design "a new generation of emergency parachutes that would work on small jets and could be steered by pilots as they drift to the ground." From "New System Saves Airplanes with Parachutes," by Associated Press, *St. Petersburg Times*, December 26, 2004.

page 93 "It's a dog. You should take it out back and shoot it." From "AOL Leads American Public Online," by Gordon Platt and Mark Johnson, *Global Finance*, January, 2005.

page 94 "People HATE spiders. [Besides,] teenagers can only be side-kicks, not superheroes." From "A Tangled Web of Deal-Making," by Michael A. Hiltzik, *Los Angeles Times*, August 29, 1998.

page 96 "People thought this idea was crazy—that consumers would rent movies through the mail." From "Does the Kid Stay in the Picture?" by Gary Rivlin, *New York Times*, February 22, 2005.

page 97 "To be doubted and be successful is particularly satisfying." From "Does the Kid Stay in the Picture?" by Gary Rivlin, *New York Times*, February 22, 2005.

page 97 "The really good idea is always traceable back quite a long way, often to a not very good idea . . . which somebody else misunderstood in such a way that they then said something which was really rather interesting." From "To Err Is Divine," by John Cleese, *Context*, Summer 1998.

page 97 Toti described his first flotation devices (filled with duck feathers) as "too bulky and heavy, so I switched to air." From "Finding an Elegant Solution," by Roger W. Hoskins, *Modesto Bee*, November 7, 2004.

page 98 "Failure is only the opportunity to begin again more intelligently." From *My Life and Work*, by Henry Ford (Kessinger Publishing, 2003).

page 98 "Writing, like life, is a voyage of discovery." From *Henry Miller on Writing*, by Henry Miller (New Directions Publishing, 1964).

page 98 "Common sense is just another name for the prejudices that we have been brought up with." From "Science in the Next Millennium," remarks by Stephen Hawking at the White House Millennium Council, 2000.

page 99 Comments about medical insurers "rethinking the traditional approach known as 'defend and deny.' " From "Medical Contrition: Doctors' New Tool to Fight Lawsuits: Saying 'I'm Sorry'," by Rachel Zimmerman, *Wall Street Journal*, May 18, 2004.

page 99 Comments about an editorial in the *Annals of Internal Medicine* suggesting that the Sorry Works program (VA Hospital, Lexington, KY) "seems to be the rare solution that is both ethically correct and cost-effective" and comments by Rick Boothman (University of Michigan Health System). From "Maybe Docs Can Just Say 'I'm Sorry'," by Jim Ritter, *Chicago Sun Times*, February 24, 2005.

page 100 "Patients are far more forgiving than we give them credit for." From "Maybe Docs Can Just Say 'I'm Sorry'," by Jim Ritter, *Chicago Sun Times*, February 24, 2005.

page 101 Rachmaninoff thought parts of his *Piano Concerto Number 2* were "absolutely repulsive." From the *Encyclopedia of the Great Composers and Their Music*, by Milton Cross (Doubleday, 1953).

page 101 Joni Mitchell originally thought "Both Sides Now" was "a failure," though she later admitted, "I was not a good judge of my early material." From "An Art Born of Pain, an Artist in Happy Exile," by Robert Hilburn, *Los Angeles Times*, September 5, 2004.

page 101 Even though the movies *In the Line of Fire* (1993) and *Places in the Heart* (1984) "turned out really well," Malkovich concludes: "The main point is that you don't know" in advance how a movie will turn out. From "Q&A: John Malkovich," by Mark Saylor, *Los Angeles Times*, June 4, 1997.

page 101 "I can finish a movie I think is great work," says Allen "and it'll end up meaning nothing to people. They think it's insipid, pretentious, stupid, and they don't come to see it. On the other hand, I'll make films I'm humiliated by . . . But people will say, 'You're wrong, it's saying something to us.' " From *Woody Allen: A Biography*, by Eric Lax (Vintage Books, 1992).

page 102 Film editor Ralph Rosenblum called the first cut of Woody Allen's *Annie Hall*, a "chaotic collection of bits and pieces that seemed to defy continuity." From *When the Shooting Stops: The Cutting Begins*, by Ralph Rosenblum (Da Capo Press, 1968).

page 102 "Just for a moment," recalled *Annie Hall* cowriter Marshall Brickman, "I had a sense of panic: we took a chance, and it didn't work; we will be humiliated; is there any way to stop the project?" From *When the Shooting Stops: The Cutting Begins*, by Ralph Rosenblum (Da Capo Press, 1968).

page 102 "Thank God," says Allen, "the public only sees the finished product." From *Woody Allen: A Biography*, by Eric Lax (Vintage Books, 1992).

page 108 "BP wanted to dramatically transform the perception of the brand, to be known worldwide as the first environmentally friendly energy company—a bold, audacious goal." From Allen Adamson, personal correspondence.

page 120 Description of Gates's annual retreat as a way to "ponder the future of technology" from "Microsoft's 'Thoreau' Takes to Woods to Ponder Future," by Robert A. Guth, *Seattle Times*, March 30, 2005.

page 122 "People always ask who influenced me the most, and I think the true answer is . . . probably all the bad films I have seen by directors whose names I promised not to remember because I would say [to myself]: 'I'm never going to do *that*.' " From *Easy Riders, Raging Bulls: How the Sex-Drugs-and-Rock 'n' Roll Generation Saved Hollywood*, by Peter Biskind (Simon & Schuster, 1999).

page 126 "As my wife walked onto the lot, and I rolled in my wheelchair. . . . Always there is a way!" From Glen McIntyre, personal correspondence.

page 127 "It wasn't working." "I started to think, 'Oh, my God, I'm going to become one of those writers who are working on the same book for ten years.' Then I started thinking, 'Well, what would that be like? Who does it happen to and why does it happen?' " From "A Life of Wonder and Awe Books," by Erik Himmelsbach, *Los Angeles Times*, April 27, 2005.

page 129 Comments by Ben and Jerry (Ben Cohen and Jerry Greenfield) from a *New York Times* magazine interview conducted by Claudia Dreifus, December 18, 1994.

page 130 "When you're forced to do something with less money, you're forced to use your imagination and things usually turn out even better." From "Moving 'Sideways' to Stay on Track," by Patrick Goldstein, *Los Angeles Times*, December 16, 2003.

page 131 "If it's sunny, people can sit outside while they wait and watch the planes take off and land." From "Smaller Airports Are Growing in Stature," by Barry Estabrook, *New York Times*, December 21, 2003.

page 133 "You buy the T-shirt at Old Navy that's good for eight weeks and, great, you throw it out. These aren't cherished pieces." From "Ikea Challenges America's 'Old-Furniture' Culture," by Stuart Elliott, *New York Times*, September 17, 2002.

page 139 The "innovation" behind FedEx came from Smith's "taking an idea from the telecommunications and banking industries, and applying that idea to the transportation business . . ." for packages that need to be delivered "absolutely, positively overnight." From "Here's an Idea!" by Jill Rosenfeld, *Fast Company*, April 2000.

page 140 "I invented nothing new. I simply assembled into a car the discoveries of other men behind whom were centuries of work." From *My Life and Work*, by Henry Ford (Kessinger Publishing, 2003).

page 144 Bette Nesmith Graham's comments about her managing to "observe people in their daily lives," "identify a need," and ". . . make a little extra money. . . . So I decided to use what artists use . . . . And I used that to correct my typing mistakes." From *Mothers of Invention*, by Ethlie Ann Vare and Greg Ptacek (William Morrow & Co., 1988).

pages 144–145 Sam Farber's recollections about the genesis of OXO, from the company's Web site, www.oxo.com.

page 145 John Kilcullen ". . . overheard a customer asking a software-store clerk for a book about DOS . . . 'something really low-level . . . DOS for dummies.' . . ." From *People*, issue date unknown.

page 145 "Don't step on my suedes." From an interview with Carl Perkins conducted by Jay Corbin in 1989 on KDHI radio (Twentynine Palms, California).

page 145 "I remember asking the chauffeur once if he was having a good week. He said, 'I'm very busy at the moment. I've been working eight days a week.' And I thought, 'Eight days a week!' Now there's a title!' " From *Paul McCartney: Many Years from Now*, by Barry Miles (Henry Holt & Company, 1997).

page 147 "One thing I have learned in a long life: that all our science, measured against reality, is primitive and childlike." From *Albert Einstein: Creator and Rebel*, by Banesh Hoffmann (Viking, 1972).

page 148 ". . . the cleanest leaf of all—the white lotus—turned out to have tiny points on it, like a bed of nails. . . . When a drop of water rolls across the tiny points, it picks up the poorly attached dirt and carries it away." From "Engineers Ask Nature for Design Advice," by Jim Robbins, *New York Times*, December 11, 2001.

page 148 "The question we ask is, *How would nature solve this problem?* . . . Can you do it without dye. . . . Can you . . . take a sliver off the top and replace that?" From "Engineers Ask Nature for Design Advice," by Jim Robbins, *New York Times*, December 11, 2001.

page 149 Poisonous ionic mercury waste left in the ground by "thirty-five former hat factories" is being cleaned up by 160 genetically-modified cottonwood trees that are "gobbling up deadly ionic mercury, metabolizing it, and then dispersing a less harmful form of elemental mercury into the atmosphere." From "The Living Machines," by Buck McMahon, *Esquire*, December 1, 2004.

page 149 Meagher confides being called a "crackpot and a charlatan." From "The Living Machines," by Buck McMahon, *Esquire*, December 1, 2004.

page 150 "[W]hat he [Maurer] calls *hasard*, the French word for chance . . . 'I wait until the moment comes . . . I don't try to force.' " "His inspiration for Ya Ya Ho (1984) . . . was born on a New Year's Eve in Haiti. . . . I could have stood there forever." From "Design Notebook; Tripping the Light Fantastically" by Patricia Leigh Brown, *New York Times*, November 26, 1998.

page 152 "All of us who came after are pretenders. . . . A night doesn't go by that I don't ask myself, 'What would Johnny [Carson] have done?' " From "The Late-Night King Kept Joking Long after His Reign Was Over," by Bill Carter, *New York Times*, January 24, 2005.

pages 152–153 "If one day I was stuck, I could ask myself, How would Martha [Graham] move? or What would [dance pioneer and choreographer] Doris Humphrey feel like? I could harness their memory as easily as if it were my own, and use the things they were using to fashion my own solutions." From *The Creative Habit: Learn It and Use It for Life*, by Twyla Tharp (Simon & Schuster, 2003).

page 153 " 'No, that would be gauche.' But then I think of Luis Alvarez, the physicist. He's a guy I admire for his gutsiness and sense of humor, and I think, 'If Alvarez was on the commission, he would do it, and that's good enough for me.' " From *What Do You Care What Other People Think? Further Adventures of a Curious Character*, by Richard P. Feynman (W. W. Norton & Company, 1988).

page 153 "When I was beginning, I would sometimes find myself solving problems in exactly the same way that teachers such as Martha Graham and Merce Cunningham solved them. I would catch myself and say, 'Wait a minute. That's how Martha or Merce would do it. We can't have that.' " She continues: "Scratching among the paradigms" is fine, unless "it turns you into an imitator rather than a creator." From *The Creative Habit: Learn It and Use It for Life*, by Twyla Tharp (Simon & Schuster, 2003).

page 153 "We don't always do what Harvey would. And in many instances we do what he wouldn't. But we all got infected by that same bug: 'Don't think small. There's no such thing as a small film, only small audiences.' " From "Weinstein's Miramax, a Crucible for Future Hollywood Leaders," by Sharon Waxman, *New York Times*, February 15, 2005.

page 154 "You should always have three things in your head that you want to say about your new movie. And you say those things no matter what you're asked." From *Los Angeles Times*, date unknown.

page 155 "Style and structure are the essence of a book; great ideas are hogwash." From *Strong Opinions*, by Vladimir Nabokov (McGraw-Hill, 1973).

pages 157–158 "The Institute for Creative Technology is the country's only organization that draws on entertainment industry know-how to sharpen military training through futuristic games and simulation" in order "to make a soldier's training more compelling." From "Coming to an Army Near You," by Dana Calvo, *Los Angeles Times*, July 19, 2002.

page 160 "Listening to your customers is a way to make a fortune." From *Selling with Honor*, by Lawrence Kohn and Joel Saltzman (Berkley Publishing Group, 1997).

page 160 "For years, Barbie dolls sold in Japan looked different from their U.S. counterparts. They had Asian facial features, black hair, and Japanese-inspired fashions. Then [around 2000] Mattel Inc. . . . learned something surprising: The original Barbie . . . played as well in Hong Kong as it did in Hollywood." From "Small World: One-Toy-Fits-All," by Lisa Bannon and Carlta Vitzhum, *Wall Street Journal*, April 29, 2003.

page 160 "We were making demos for what was our third album in Sayreville, N.J.—my hometown—in a little demo studio. . . . I went around the corner to have a pizza, and a bunch of kids were in there, and they said we know you guys, you made two records. . . . So we invited a dozen of them back and their reaction to various songs helped influence the decision making." From "Soul Proprietor: Jon Bon Jovi," by Adam Hanft, *Inc.*, June 1, 2004.

page 163 "Every time we design a new airplane, we come up with ideas that make us slap ourselves on the forehead and ask, 'Why didn't we think of that before?' " From "Boeing's New Baby," by J. Lynn Lunsford, *Wall Street Journal*, November 18, 2003.

page 167 Fisher recommends a 15 percent tax on the purchase of "devices used for storing and copying music and movies—like CD burners, MP3 players, and blank CDs." From *Promises to Keep: Technology, Law, and the Future of Entertainment*, by William W. Fisher III (Stanford University Press, 2004).

page 173 "I keep a notebook in my pocket at all time[s] . . . Good ideas come from people everywhere, not in the boardroom." From "26 Most Fascinating Entrepreneurs," by Michael S. Hopkins, *Inc.*, April 2005.

page 173 "Ideas are a dime a dozen. People who implement them are priceless." From *Mary Kay: You Can Have It All: Lifetime Wisdom from America's Foremost Woman Entrepreneur*, by Mary Kay Ash (Prima Lifestyles, 1995).

page 175 "Rollerblading; in Hawaii; when I'm hanging out and chatting with friends. Anywhere but the office." From *They Made America*, by Harold Evans (Little Brown, 2004).

pages 175–176 "Disgusted with my failure [to solve some mathematical questions], I went to spend a few days at the seaside, and thought of something else. . . . that the arithmetic forms were identical with those of non-Euclidean geometry." From "The Foundations of Science," by Henri Poincaré, first published in Paris in 1908. Available in *The Value of Science: Essential Writings of Henri Poincaré* (Modern Library, 2001).

page 176 "Taking a break . . . gives you stuff to draw on, gives you inspiration." From *If You Can Talk, You Can Write*, by Joel Saltzman (Warner Books, 1997).

page 176 "You go back to it and you suddenly see something that if you'd been rushing and pushing you wouldn't have seen it." From *If You Can Talk, You Can Write*, by Joel Saltzman (Warner Books, 1997).

page 177 "It was a big weight off my shoulders. . . . Then out of the blue . . . like tumblers clicking successively into place on a safe: Act I, Act II, Act III. Don't know why, don't know where it came from." From "A Rare Screen Test for Phillip Roth," by Barbara Kantrowitz, *New York Times*, August 11, 2002.

page 181 "We only have 10 percent of the market, and that means that 90 percent of the women are buying the wrong cosmetics." From *Mary Kay: You Can Have It All: Lifetime Wisdom from America's Foremost Woman Entrepreneur*, by Mary Kay Ash (Prima Lifestyles, 1995).

page 181 Telegraph operators would soon "transmit the sound of their own voices over the wire, and talk with one another instead of telegraphing." As reported in *They All Laughed . . . From Light Bulbs to Lasers: The Fascinating Stories Behind the Great Inventions That Have Changed Our Lives*, by Ira Flatow (HarperCollins, 1992).

page 183 He "wrote forward-looking white papers such as 'Computers by the Millions' so that management could see what the computing world would be like in the coming decade." From "Jeff Raskin, the Visionary Behind the Mac," from an interview with Raskin conducted by Jason Walsh appearing in *LowEnd-Mac.com*, January 19, 2005.

page 184 "All of our IQ's would have been 10 points lower, on account of all the lead in the air." From "The Big Awards Show," by Lee Gomes, *Wall Street Journal*, March 1, 2004.

page 185 On Hovey describing Walgreens as "the mouse parts store." From "Mighty Mouse," by Alex Soojung-Kim Pang, *Stanford Magazine*, March/April 2002.

page 186 "Commit your blunders on a small scale, and make your profits on a large scale." From *They Made America*, by Harold Evans (Little Brown, 2004).

page 189 "I imagine you can't even see the fish." Land's demonstration of glare-reducing Polaroid lenses. From *They Made America*, by Harold Evans (Little Brown, 2004)

page 192 " 'How about something slimy, like a python?' And then Eric [Idle] said something about a seedy music hall agent named Monty. And we all said, 'That's it!' " From "Something Completely Nostalgic; A Monty Python Reunion, Minus One Slapstick Subversive," by Bruce Weber, *New York Times*, March 9, 1998.

page 193 "We lost track of how many times we heard No." From "Entrepreneur of the Year," by Anne Murphy, *Inc.*, December 1995.

page 194 "I lose most of the time. For me, losing is just learning how to win." From *Selling With Honor*, by Lawrence Kohn and Joel Saltzman (Berkley Publishing Group, 1997).

About the Author

Joel Saltzman is the creator of the *Shake That Brain!*® system—for winning solutions AND lots of fun. A high-octane speaker, facilitator, and consultant, Joel helps organizations discover extraordinary solutions for marketing, innovation, building better teams, and improving the bottom line. The author of more than a dozen books—including four best sellers—all his work has one thing in common: creative solutions.

His first book, *If You Can Talk, You Can Write*, became a best seller for Warner Books and a selection of the Quality Paperback Book Club. In 2000, his audio recording of the book won him a national Audie Award for "Best Educational and Training Audio."

As J. S. Salt, he created the best seller, *Always Kiss Me Good Night: Instructions on Raising The Perfect Parent by 147 Kids Who Know* (Random House, 1997).

The founder and publisher of *Shake It!* Books, he created and marketed the popular series, *How To Be The Almost Perfect Husband: By Wives Who Know* and *How To Be The Almost Perfect Wife: By Husbands Who Know* (Shake It! Books, 2000).

Joel began his career in New York with the advertising agency Young & Rubicam. Moving to Hollywood, he wrote sitcoms for *Perfect Strangers* and *The Robert Guillaume Show*. He also served time as a stand-up comedian.

He's been a guest on *Leeza* (twice) and has been interviewed on CNN, NPR, and more than 500 radio shows. A graduate of

Cornell University, Joel lives with his wife, son, and Tux-the-Wonder-Dog in San Diego, California.

www.**shake**that**brain**.com

joel@**shake**that**brain**.com

Toll Free: (877) Shake It! (877-742-5348)

Index